HERE'S WHAT READERS SAID ABOUT THE FIRST EDITION OF
Making Big Money Investing in Foreclosures Without Cash or Credit:

Michael King

I knew that there was more to life than a *job* and I could achieve it if I was willing to make the effort. The greatest satisfaction for me comes from taking a house that is trashed and turning it into a desirable home. To do the same, read Peter's *Making Big Money in Foreclosures* and study your area and market well. Then find ways to hang out with other winners like those you'd find in The Mentor Family.

Teri Darnell

Although I've always had a good job and made decent money, living is expensive. But it's very easy to refinance and continue to borrow until one day you realize you're in way over your head. I was in foreclosure myself in the early '90s, so I understand the mental state people are in when it's happening. When money is short, it's so easy to leave your bills unopened and stick your head in the sand. It's a state of denial.

Today, I'm able to tell people my story and show them I'm a living example of life after foreclosure. I've been there, done that, and have bought real estate many times since, so it's not the end but a new beginning.

JJ Bergstrom

I thought this was a business for scoundrels, but that isn't the case. The "used-car salesman" types are not going to make it because they only care about the deal. Care about the people; be honest and ethical in everything you do.

Carol Cunningham

I bought a home from a couple who was getting a divorce. The house was going into foreclosure. I hired a contractor to make repairs. I painted it and brought in new appliances and lighting. I sold the house three months later to the first person who walked in the door for a profit of $25,000! My success enabled me to purchase a new home for my personal residence. We have taken vacations we would have never experienced otherwise. If you don't believe in your own success, you'll never take the first step.

Steve Faulkner

I was tired of working in corporate America and traveling a hundred nights a year. I left a $70,000 a year job with a company car, expenses, and all that to build my real estate business. The breaking point came when my three-year-old daughter told my wife that she wanted to go to Daddy's house. My wife assured her that I lived in our house, but she was convinced that I lived in Oklahoma City and just came to see them on weekends. Now my 14-year-old son can go to work with me, and I'm home every night.

We developed a relationship with several real estate agents who give us first shot at a lot of real estate owned (REO) properties before they go out to the MLS. They like it because there's no commission split. We have done 17 houses this year so far with 5 from these agents. The secret to establishing good relationships with real estate agents is successfully delivering fast closings and doing what we said we would.

We made $98,000 from foreclosures this year, plus $19,000 in nonrefundable option payments and $1,907 monthly positive cash flow from rental income. Don't be afraid; this isn't rocket science. Get the Mentorship Program training and use it!

Aaron Murphy

The biggest obstacle I had to overcome was "analysis paralysis." Get educated. Find a home study course and/or mentor that you've researched and believe in. But don't WAIT once you've been educated. You'll learn on the job, so just get going!

Since December of 2005, we have purchased one property a month. We are averaging about 75 cents on the dollar for buy versus after-repaired value. Our last two purchases were nonauction, pre-foreclosure buys at 39 cents ($76,900 buy on home worth $209,000 after fixup) and 54 cents ($211,400 on home worth $389,000). My partner and I now own approximately $2 million in real estate at age 32. I joke with my wife that even at 5 percent appreciation, my half of that growth more than covers the master's in social work salary she had been making, and she gets to stay home with our son. That is a true measure of early success!

Ed Stigall

I'm a 74-year-old retired real estate broker. I retired after 35 years but was bored with retirement. I jumped into foreclosure real estate, and I love it! I read Peter's book on investing in foreclosures. I attended the Ultimate Investors Bootcamp training with The Success Team in Denver in May 2006. I started mailing letters and calling foreclosures about that time and subscribed to two foreclosure websites. Now business is growing because I'm finding that people will really deed their property over to me! My advice is to get good training and believe that you can do it.

Ellen Denler

We started with one little two-bedroom REO house that we bought for $30,000. We turned it into a three-bedroom house and sold it for $77,500. It took us a year and a half, but we did make $10,000 on it. *Making Big Money Investing in Foreclosures* made us realize we didn't have to use "our" money. We have the use of private money or somebody else's money when we do wholesaling. So I guess fear was the biggest thing to overcome. We also had to develop the confidence to just do it!

Gene Yandell

I've been investing for three years, and I own 9 properties (18 rental units). I have a mix of single-family homes, fourplexes, and vacation properties. To date, I have purchased $3.5 million in real estate. Getting laid off was the push I needed to get started. After reading some other success-oriented books, I learned about Peter Conti and The Mentor Family. Their investment advice supports everything that I have read from Robert Kiyosaki and Diane Kennedy. I am looking forward to my next deals and see them likely coming from foreclosures.

James Best

I started by buying VA foreclosures and lease optioning them. I then started finding people who needed to sell their homes and offering solutions to their problems. The biggest obstacle was convincing my wife that this was a good and profitable business. She is convinced now after seeing the people we helped and receiving the big checks. We close on a house next week that will net $150,000.

I think the most important thing is to go out there and apply the knowledge you have gotten from the books, tapes, and boot camps. Do not be afraid to make a mistake. I have found that real estate is usually very forgiving.

M. A. Wallinger

Within 10 years of retirement, I decided to get into real estate as part of my retirement plan. I taught my family what I was learning so that they could enjoy the benefits of real estate investing, too. I am currently working with a homeowner facing foreclosure who is upside down in the property and ready to just walk away from it. If we are successful in arranging a short sale with her mortgage company, I not only will help this owner by stopping the foreclosure, but my projected net profit from selling on a rent-to-own basis will be around $50,000.

Mary Parker

I had always wanted to invest in real estate, but health problems kept me from pursuing it. Our monthly bills ranged from $8,500 to $10,000, and we had no money coming in. I studied and read information about buying foreclosures, including Peter's book. I started advertising to buy foreclosure properties, and we bought our first property and rehabbed it. I closed seven weeks later and made $30,000. I became successful by putting up Bandit signs repeatedly, advertising in our local papers, and purchasing billboards. I knew that to make at least $10,000 a month, I had to use a variety of advertising. I also purchase our local foreclosure information published weekly online, and I constantly send mailings and knock on doors of those people whose houses are in the foreclosure market.

Making Big Money Investing in Foreclosures

WITHOUT CASH OR CREDIT

2nd Edition

by Peter Conti

PUBLISHING

New York

Vice President and Publisher: Maureen McMahon
Editorial Director: Jennifer Farthing
Development Editor: Joshua Martino
Production Editor: Fred Urfer
Production Artist: Areta Buk
Cover Designer: Rod Hernandez

Published by Kaplan Publishing,
a division of Kaplan, Inc.

Printed in the United States of America

June 2007

07 08 09   10 9 8 7 6 5 4 3 2 1

ISBN 13: 978-1-4195-9722-0

Kaplan Publishing books are available at special quantity discounts to use for sales promotions, employee premiums, or educational purposes. Please email our Special Sales Department to order or for more information at kaplanpublishing@kaplan.com, or write to Kaplan Publishing, 1 Liberty Plaza, 24th Floor, NY, NY 10006.

To Noni—You succeeded even with the odds stacked against you. Thanks for showing me what's possible. I know that you will get this message.

Peter Conti

C ontents

One of the first things I noticed about Peter Conti was the concern he had for new students. When I asked him about it, he said he worried about people getting started. He knew from experience that "making it" in the foreclosure business requires more than getting educated. He was encouraged by seeing a handful of students decide on their own to create in-person peer groups with other highly driven people. I remember Peter's saying, "I don't think that the Internet can provide the sense of connection that everyone seems to be so hungry for today."

I had the chance to work directly with Peter to jump-start the Commercial Real Estate Mentoring Program. I saw firsthand how clients applied the techniques and philosophies described in this book to work everyday miracles with their investing. I also watched Peter build what he now calls The Mentor Family™, a system and gathering place for investors to share their successes and their failures. These are providing the connections investors are hungry for.

I know that Peter believes (as I do) that if you want to get ahead, you've got to be willing to fall down and be taught how to stand up again. His passion for teaching and encouraging people to reach for a better life through real estate is contagious. The proof of his willingness to teach his investing methods rests with the transformed students I meet everywhere I go.

Peter, thank you for being my friend as well as an incredible partner. You'll never know the number of lives you have influenced.

All my best,

Peter Harris, coauthor *Investing in Multi-Units* with Donald Trump

Our students would not have been able to create the amazing results and open up new possibilities in their lives without the support from the entire Success Team at Mentor Financial Group. Special thanks to our Success Team Coaches and other Success Team Members.

All of our Success Team Coaches:

Robb Novak	Stephen Wilklow
Rob Powell	Juli Butler
Emily Cressey	Cleve Schenck
Cheryl Hastings	Peter Harris
Mike Ouellette	

Other Success Team Members:

Angela Hensiek	Elaine Morris
Jeff Hensiek	Denise Czarnecki
Marilyn Rhodes	Christiana Cha
Deb Williams	Kevin Orlowski
Elizabeth Carter	Linda Wheeler
Laura Macomber	Thomas Mangum
Amy Turpin	Kurt Frank

Special thanks to the experts at Kaplan Publishing, who not only have done much to make *Making Big Money Investing in Real Estate Without Tenants, Banks, or Rehab Projects* as well as the first edition of *Making Big Money Investing in Foreclosures* such a huge success but who put in much effort to make this book a useful tool to foreclosure investors. Barbara McNichol—you are a wonderful editor. Thanks for working with us to make this book the best it could be. And thanks to Jennifer Farthing, acquisitions editor at Kaplan Publishing, who guided the project along.

Our final thank-you goes to you, our investors and clients. When an email went out asking you to share stories about foreclosure deals, we were flooded with responses. We are humbled by your generosity. We had everyone in the office reading about your experiences and were touched by your willingness to trust us as we welcomed you into the The Mentor Family™. Whether you join us a for a free trial after reading this book, have taken one of our online training courses, bought foreclosures with us in The Mentorship Program, or gone on to join the Commercial Real Estate Mentoring Program, we believe in you and your ability to impact the world in a positive way.

FROM THE DESK OF PETER CONTI

Thank you for taking the time to pick up this newest revised version of our *Wall Street Journal* best-selling book, *Making Big Money in Foreclosures Without Cash or Credit.* You, the reader, can be thanked for the success of this book. You have seen there is a lot of great information in this book, or else you wouldn't have referred it to all of your friends and colleagues and everyone you've met at your local Real Estate Investors Association meetings.

As you read through this book, you'll see several new things that you haven't seen before. Let's take a moment here to introduce them to you. Don't get me wrong; the first edition is packed full of information that is still pertinent. However, as the foreclosure investing market grows and changes, I wanted to share the latest changes with you as well.

Over the past 10+ years, Mentor Financial Group, LLC, has grown and changed so much that it really has become a family. When our company started, I never dreamed that we'd impact so many people's lives. Here's what this wonderful experience and a great family of investors has grown into.

The Mentor Family™—Several times throughout this book, we'll be talking about students in our Mentor Family. This is a select group of students who have gone through an extensive selection process and have been handpicked to be among the best investors in the United States. These are some of my closest friends, colleagues, and associates. I really enjoy working with each of these students, hearing their success stories, and watching them grow into being amazing investors whom I have personally trained and continue to mentor.

New Success Team Stories—In the first edition, all of the stories came from my experience and from the experiences of our students. I've discovered that successful investors who have a passion to teach can be hard to hold back. Many students have grown over time to become full-time investors and part-time coaches for the The Mentor Family™ in our Mentorship Program. So throughout this book, you'll not only hear stories from me but also from some of the amazing students and coaches who themselves have changed their lives through real estate.

Mentorship Program—You'll read throughout this revision about students in our Mentorship Program. As the world of real estate changes, we, as investors, need to adapt as well. Applying the concept of investing from the heart has always been at the core of our students, coaches, and staff. As a result, we have clearly identified why we feel we are uniquely different from any other group of investors or training, and thus—the Mentorship Program.

Let's be clear on one thing: investing in real estate is an area in which you have a choice. You can either be an honest, upright, straightforward investor who chooses to work ethically and honestly within the law—or you can be swayed to the other direction. If you see someone who puts profits ahead of everything else, please don't mention this book or suggest that they go to our website or training sessions. I've discovered that the type of client that becomes part of The Mentor Family™ chooses to use this book and the concepts in this book to transform their life and the lives of everyone they touch. And by following in the paths of others who believe as you do, you'll find that it's actually much easier to do it the right way.

Taking It All the Way to the Bank—Plenty of people get stuck on the way to being successful. They think they have to learn every last detail before they get started. By joining us in reading this book, we're going to expect more from you. For example, as part of our Mentorship Program, we take two deals "all the way to the bank" with our students. This includes the entire process—not just finding the deal, negotiating it, and structuring it but well beyond that. That includes the boring but important details like getting all the paperwork done correctly. We've discovered that real success is defined by results. For this type of family member, we define success as taking two deals all the way to completion and actually putting the check in the bank.

The least that we're going to expect from you is that you agree to go out and apply the ideas that you learn in this book. Don't worry: we've provided a simple action plan in the last chapter along with some online resources to point you in the right direction.

These are just a few of the many additions to this book that I am very excited to be able to present to you. Look for these key concepts scattered through out the book. Let's get started with sharing with you how:

You Can Earn Up to an Extra $100,000 This Year in Foreclosures

1

YOU CAN EARN
UP TO AN EXTRA
$100,000 THIS YEAR
IN FORECLOSURES

Three years ago, Sarah, in her forties, went from being a highly paid executive during the dot-com boom to an out-of-work statistic in the dot-com bust. Whether you're an executive in the corporate world, a professional person with your own business, or a blue-collar worker with dirt under your fingernails, you can imagine how scary that was for Sarah. Nothing she had learned over the previous 15 years of corporate life had prepared her for the harsh realities of being on her own.

Sarah vowed that never again would she depend on a job or corporation for her income. She decided to start investing in real estate. A few months after she made this decision, she came to a workshop we hosted in San Diego. She sat right in the front row and took page after page of notes. Hungry to learn how to build wealth by starting up a real estate investing business, she asked probing questions at every break. How did things turn out for Sarah?

During her first 12 months of investing, she completed 10 deals and earned more than $150,000 net profit. Today, she specializes in buying preforeclosures and foreclosure properties in her hometown and earns a lot more money than when she first started investing.

I'm not going to tell you she had it easy—just as many of you won't have it easy—but it can be done. And *you* are the one who can do it.

Over the past decade, as part of the Mentor Family, I've been blessed to have helped launch the investing careers of thousands of people across the country who, just like you, picked up a copy of this simple book and began a journey that continues to this day. In fact, over that time, our students have bought and sold more than $1 *billion* of real estate. We know we live in a cynical world in which friends and family may say it can't be done. But we're here to tell you that if tens of thousands of our students can do it, you can too.

Mark, a pilot for a large commercial airline, made more than $100,000 from his first foreclosure deal. His greatest dream was to make enough money with his real estate investing that he could quit his airline job and teach high school band classes. Music was his passion and his drive. Mark has now completed many more deals and created a whole new life for himself. If he can have the courage to successfully chase his dreams, you can too.

Laura, a nineteen-year-old woman, was recovering from a broken back when she first began learning about investing. She spent two months listening to borrowed investing course tapes and reading investing books as she convalesced. Two months later, she bought her first investment property and was off and running. Five years later, her real estate business generates $40,000 a month of gross revenue, and her net worth is $1.5 million. If this young woman with no experience can find a way to become successful, so can you.

Randy is a beginning investor from Hawaii. He finally found his answer for all those people who kept telling him "it couldn't be done" when he made more than $60,000 on his first foreclosure deal. If Randy can ignore negative influences and realize a huge new world of opportunity, you can too.

Michael learned that his company was about to lay him off. With a wife who was pregnant with their first child, this was a major wake-up call for him. While Michael's company decided not to lay him off, he swore that he would never put himself and his family in a financial position that vulnerable again. That was when he came across the first edition of this book. In his first year of investing, he followed the systematic advice and strategies you'll learn about in these chapters. Michael completed eight deals and made $405,000 in cash profits. You, too, can use the same strategies as your proven wealth vehicle to take back control over your own financial future and become financially free. Michael is now also one of my coaches for our Mentorship Program.

WHY THE TIME IS NOW

There has never been a better time to take control of your financial destiny and get out of the rat race. All across the United States, foreclosure rates are climbing like rockets and bursting onto investors' radar screens. Now is the time to cash in on these unprecedented bargains for yourself and help other people at the same time. Don't miss out on big opportunities to make money investing in foreclosures.

The following indicators have helped drive the foreclosure rate up more than 400 percent over the past 30 years in the United States. And it's only getting higher.

Personal bankruptcy rates are up 400 percent from what they were 40 years ago. Gambling as a percentage of the average person's disposable income has increased by more than 700 percent over the past 40 years. In fact, online gambling has *doubled* in the last 12 months! Consumer debt is at an historic high, while savings rates are at historic lows. For the past 30 years, the number of people not covered by health insurance has climbed above 50 percent. (Source: Federal Deposit Insurance Corporation Division of Research and Statistics)

According to the Mortgage Bankers Association of America, 4.41 percent of all residential housing was in various stages of preforeclosure or foreclosure by the end of August 2006. This number has doubled over the past several years. That rate is even higher when you look at subprime and FHA loans, which both had delinquency rates of roughly 12 percent as of the first quarter of 2006. Twelve percent! And these rates are climbing.

The next time you drive to your local supermarket to shop, you'll probably pass 1,000 homes. Of these, statistically speaking, 44 are in preforeclosure or foreclosure. That means in your neighborhood within a few minutes' walk, four to five of your neighbors are delinquent on their loans and in danger of losing their homes to foreclosure. These people need your help. And as you help them, you'll earn a healthy profit.

WHY FORECLOSURE RATES KEEP CLIMBING

Only four decades ago, to get a loan to buy a home, a borrower needed a 20 percent down payment, strong credit, and stable income that was at least three times the mortgage payments. But the world has changed, and so has the lending market.

Today, home buyers can get zero-down loans with adjustable-rate mortgages that actually cause their loan balances to increase every month (called *negative amortizing loans*). In fact, lenders today have loosened up their requirements on credit standards (witness the explosion of subprime loans) and income levels (with many lenders requiring only twice the income of the total home monthly payment).

TOXIC MORTGAGES

A recent (September 6, 2006) *Business Week* cover asked, "How Toxic Is Your Mortgage?" The 14-page feature article inside reported on the alarming rise in "option ARM loans." These are adjustable-rate mortgages that offer several payment options to the borrower, including one option, called the "minimum payment," which is less than the cost of the interest so that the loan grows bigger every month. According to this article, up to 80 percent of all option ARM borrowers make only the minimum payment!

In 2005, Countrywide Home Mortgage (the nation's number one mortgage lender) had a *500 percent increase* in option ARM loans. According to the article, more than 20 percent of all option ARM loans in 2004 and 2005 were worth less than the outstanding loan balance. And if the real estate market fell by just 10 percent, that number would double to 40 percent!

And if that wasn't enough, in 2005, lenders gave 43 percent of first-time buyers loans for 100 percent of the purchase price (Source: National Association of REALTORS®). That left these homeowners vulnerable to the slightest economic quiver.

A SHIFT IN THE REAL ESTATE MARKET

The headlines are everywhere. In the summer (August 26) of 2006, the cover of *The Economist* asked "Has America's Housing Bubble Burst?" That same year, *USA Today* reported about the declining real estate market. What's happening?

The answer is that another cycle is playing out in the real estate market. From 2000 to 2005, the total value of American homes skyrocketed from $9 trillion to $22 trillion. However, this huge growth of real estate has slowed down drastically. In many parts of the country, especially the Midwest, real estate is declining in value.

When you add this decline in the real estate market to decade-long loose-lending trends, you get a recipe for a massive increase in opportunities for foreclosure investors.

HOW TO INVEST IN TODAY'S CHANGING MARKET CONDITIONS

Prudent investors have always known that you can make a lot of money investing in real estate in any market. And if you stick with your investing for long enough, most likely you'll get the chance to invest in every kind of market—from depreciating markets where home values are dropping to flat markets where prices remain stagnant to boom markets that may be appreciating 10 percent to 20 percent (or more) a year.

With the strong fundamentals you'll read about in this book, you'll learn exactly how to profit in *each* of these types of markets. But if you expect these profits to come overnight and without a lot of hard work, you're fooling yourself. Making a ton of money investing in foreclosures may be simple, but it isn't easy. It will take energy and work on your part—first to master the skills and strategies involved and later to apply what you are learning in the real world.

TWO KEYS TO PROFITING IN ANY TYPE OF MARKET

1. *You make your profit when you buy, not when you sell.* If you are buying for cash and plan to resell the property immediately for a quick cash profit, then make sure you are buying at the right price. (You'll learn the exact formula in Chapter 3.) The secret to selling quickly is making sure that you buy low enough for the next person to make a profit. Normally if you are wholesaling the deal (Chapter 7), this

means you are buying at about 50 percent to 60 percent of market value and selling quickly at 65 percent to 70 percent of value. If you plan on selling to a retail buyer, you'll still need to be buying cheaply enough to allow yourself a big enough profit margin to cover all the rehab and holding costs until you sell. In a softening market, this may take six months or longer. This needs to be factored into your buying price.

2. *If you plan to hold the property over time, make sure the property can afford to pay for itself.* One way intelligent investors build a margin of safety into their real estate deals is by making sure they have a cash flow cushion from the start. That way, if a shift occurs in the rental market, you are insulated and can painlessly ride out the market cycle to sunnier days.

Does it make sense that, as an investor, you are going to need to create profitable deals in any market? In down markets, you need to be more discerning about which of the many deals you take. In a strong market, you need to work harder to find motivated sellers who want to work with you. The key is to adjust your investing efforts depending on the type of market you are facing.

THE REAL DIFFERENCE BETWEEN SPECULATORS AND INVESTORS

Speculators are people who buy real estate at close to—or even at—full price as part of a cash deal, and then they hope-pray-gamble the market will rapidly appreciate so they can resell the property at a profit. They are totally dependent on outside market conditions to produce a profit.

But what if the market cools off? The speculator always runs the risk of getting stuck with a property that is a "dog." Investors are smarter than that. When they buy a property, they do so knowing they are *guaranteed* to make a profit because of the way they purchased it. Either they have received great terms that generate strong cash flow, or they have negotiated a discounted cash price that ensures a profit when they resell. *The key distinction is that speculators gamble on outside forces to create a profit for themselves, while investors negotiate the price or terms they need to build into their profit from day one—no matter what the market does in the short run.*

THREE BIGGEST MYTHS ABOUT INVESTING IN FORECLOSURES

All of our lives, well-intentioned people have stated reason after reason why we can't or shouldn't make money investing in foreclosures. But what they told you was only half-true and fully misleading. They passed on their beliefs without even understanding themselves how costly these myths could be for you.

Myth #1: It Takes Money to Make Money

There you are, sitting in your family's dining room after enjoying a full holiday meal. You're a young child; your family is gathered and talking about life. How many times did you see the dreamer in your family get his or her dreams shot down with a bullet like, "You can't do that. Where will you get the money to do it?"

Were *you* the dreamer in your family who felt the sharp stab from those well-intentioned remarks? Did people who influenced you keep drilling into your head, "It takes money to make money"? Where is this myth written in stone? And if it were really true, how did people like Warren Buffett and Bill Gates start with nothing and build net worths of billions of dollars?

■ **Success Team—Peter's Story**

"I started investing while I was an auto mechanic working for less than $15 an hour. Not only didn't I have a large chunk of investing capital to start with, but my wife and I had two small kids at the time. In the home where I grew up, my dad had to work really hard to provide for his wife and seven kids. One day, I reached an emotional low when my boss yelled at me for helping myself to some coffee that he'd set out for customers. That incident gave me the courage to find a way to make investing work for me. Sometimes it does take an emotional low to help you commit to never settling for less again.   ■

 ■ **Success Team—Coach Emily's Story**

When I started investing in real estate, I had just graduated from college. I was looking for a way to succeed in life without having to work for a big corporation for 40 years. I was scrimping by on my small savings because I wanted to prove to my parents that I really could make it on my own. That's when I first got started with my investing. Over the next two years, I bought dozens of properties using other people's money and have been involved in hundreds of deals since. If a new college graduate like me can start with nothing and become a real estate millionaire in less than four years, then you can do the same thing!   ■

It doesn't take money to make money. It takes specialized knowledge of a profitable niche that you apply with disciplined and passionate efforts over time, taking care to learn and to improve along the way. Even if it really *did* take money to make money (which it doesn't), no one said it takes *your own* money to make money.

One of the advantages of investing in foreclosures is that it's easy to use other people's money to make money. You can potentially tap into thousands of dollars in profits created through buying properties using other sources of funding.

Myth #2: You Need Good Credit to Borrow Money

We can hear you saying, "Yeah, but we need good credit to borrow money so we can make money investing in foreclosures." This is true if your only source of funding is from traditional lenders. In this book, you'll learn seven other ways to fund your way into a deal with someone else's money—no matter what your credit is like.

■ **Success Team—Peter's Story**

I've had a hand in hundreds of real estate deals—acquiring interest in millions of dollars worth of real estate—yet I've only applied for funds through a conventional lender for a small handful of loans in all those years. If I can do this, you can too. It's just a matter of learning the real-world secrets that successful investors have mastered.

For example, I bought and made more than $250,000 in profits from a five-bedroom, three-and-a-half-bath house. The seller agreed to act as my bank and carry back all the financing I needed to buy that property after a small down payment. He carried back over $400,000 without ever once asking to check my credit. Was the seller unsophisticated? Was I taking advantage of him? No. He had a net worth several times greater than mine (he was a real estate investor in his seventies and I was just 38 years old at the time). He simply regarded this as a win-win situation.   ■

When you understand and apply the ideas in this book, you'll learn that motivated sellers don't care about your credit; they don't care about your home life; they don't care about *you*, period. *They care about getting out of tough situations and relieving themselves of major sources of pain in their lives.* And sellers are only one of several funding sources for your foreclosure deals.

Myth #3: If You Buy a Property from a Seller in Foreclosure, You're a Shark Taking Advantage of Another Person's Misery

This false belief would have you believe that you are out there swindling sellers by sneaking into their home, fooling them into signing documents, and running away with all their cash before they wake up to what you're doing. Far from it!

Even if some investors do business that way, let's make it absolutely clear: that's *not* how members of the Mentor Family do business. The Mentor Family is a group of our clients and readers who've discovered that real estate is about more than just making money. You see, when you help sellers in foreclosure, they are thankful for your taking time to understand their situations and finding a win-win way to solve a problem they're embarrassed and scared to admit they even have.

Investing in foreclosures is like holding the core of your being up to a mirror. If you are a good person, what reflects back is that you help people and get paid well for doing it. Isn't that what business is all about—providing value and getting paid handsomely for it?

■ **Success Team—Peter's Story**

When I think about everything I've accomplished in my life, the things that really stand out aren't the number of properties I have purchased or the wealth I have accumulated. Rather, it's what that financial wealth has enabled me to do and the people I have been able to help.

I remember Fred and Evelyn who wanted to sell their house. I recall sitting in their gorgeous home on a great lot. The house seemed perfect, but the property never sold. So Fred and Evelyn called me and we sat down at their kitchen table. Fred was doing all of the talking. It took a long time, but he finally felt comfortable enough with me to share their concerns about selling the house. They had received offers on the property, but all of the offers felt cold to them. No one had ever taken the time to sit down and really understand them. Sadly, a short time before this, their son had drowned while playing in the creek toward the back of their yard. It was important for them to share that and have someone show interest.

Fred and especially Evelyn were able to move on with their lives as a result of our conversation around that kitchen table. It emphasizes that when you invest in foreclosures, you find yourself talking with the sellers at a critical time in their lives. So take the time to listen. And realize that the connections you make with sellers and the connections you make with other investors who have the same mindset as you do are an important part of what we do as real estate investors. ■

THE CHOICE IS YOURS

When we tell people, "Anyone can make big money investing in foreclosures," most simply shake their heads and walk away. We watch them passing on what might be their best chance to create security and freedom for themselves and their families while they help people like Fred and Evelyn. They simply don't believe—or can't believe—that they could be successful this way. They say they don't have enough money, or that they don't know how, or that it's too hard. Sadly, many let themselves sink into the "lives driven by fear and obligation" that so many people lead.

But you're different. Something inside made you realize it's possible *for you* to create a life driven by passion and purpose, a possibility fueled by creating your fortune with real estate. You may not have all the know-how yet, but with the specialized knowledge you'll gain from reading this book, you'll uncover dozens of ways to find profitable foreclosure deals and structure them without using your cash or credit.

We know this sounds too good to be true. But success takes a great deal of study, disciplined action, and willingness to set aside many deeply rooted beliefs you have about wealth. If you are willing to add these three ingredients to the recipes explained in this book, we guarantee you *can* and *will* make big money investing in foreclosures.

THE BIG PICTURE OF INVESTING IN FORECLOSURES

Investing in foreclosures and preforeclosures has proven to be a rewarding and profitable niche for investors who know what they're doing. Anyone with the right attitude, the specialized knowledge, and the willingness to practice and learn along the way can make money investing in foreclosures.

This chapter defines *foreclosure*, explains the concepts involved when buying foreclosures, and walks you through several sample deals. It includes examples of how other investors have made healthy profits structuring deals with sellers of foreclosure and preforeclosure properties.

As you read through these stories, do your best to get a feel for how these deals flow and the common elements among them. Chapter 3 explains how to structure each type of these deals. For the moment, though, it's important to understand that you *can* make money buying foreclosures without cash or credit.

FORECLOSURE DEFINED

Foreclosure is the legal process by which a person or institution that is owed money can force the sale of a property to pay off the money that a borrower owes. Before getting deeper into the process, let's introduce some of the key players in the foreclosure game.

Bankers

When people go to a bank to borrow money, they're asked to sign two important documents: a *promissory note* and a security instrument (either a *deed of trust* or a *mortgage*).

The promissory note is the IOU or acknowledgment of debt. It says the borrower owes the bank a specific amount of money and lists the exact terms of the loan and the required repayment.

Imagine you were an officer at the bank. Would you give applicants $300,000 based on their word alone? Wouldn't you want a guarantee that you would indeed get your money back? This guarantee is the security instrument, which will be either a deed of trust or a mortgage, depending on where you're investing.

However, the deed of trust or mortgage is *not* an IOU or a promissory note; it is a security agreement. It states that the borrower will repay the loan and live up to the terms and conditions of the loan, or the lender can force the sale of the property to raise the money to pay for as much of the outstanding loan as possible.

Think about it this way. The loan process is like a teenager asking his parents for permission to borrow the car Saturday night. The teenager gives his best pleading performance to borrow the car saying, "Please, Mom and Dad. I want to take Sally out to the movies. I've always been responsible when you let me borrow the car in the past. . . ." Just as the teenager tries to convince his parents to lend him the car, so do loan applicants present the best possible case of their ability to repay the loan. They even show proof of their good credit history (like the teenager declaring to his parents, "I've always been responsible in the past").

Finally, the parents give in and grant permission for the teenager to borrow the car, *but* they lay down certain ground rules the teenager must follow: He must be home by 11:00 PM; he must tell them exactly where he is going, with whom, and when. Setting out the rules for lending the car is what a banker does in a promissory note—including specific terms and conditions of the loan and how and when it will be repaid.

But smart parents, just like smart bankers, know they also need to establish the consequences of what will happen if the teenager doesn't live up to his side of the agreement. "If you're not home by 11:00 PM, or if you change your plans without getting our approval first, or if you are reckless with the car, then you will be grounded and lose all car privileges for a period of time." Bankers establish consequences too, although they take it about ten steps further. They make the borrower sign a deed of trust or mortgage, which establishes the negative consequences if the borrower doesn't live up to all the terms and conditions of the promissory note.

The language in the deed of trust or mortgage says, for example, that the borrower agrees to keep the property properly insured, agrees to properly maintain the property, and, of course, agrees to make timely payments on the promissory note. If the borrower doesn't live up to these terms, then bankers apply the consequences stated in the deed of trust or mortgage—specifically, they foreclose on the house.

WHAT FORECLOSURE DEALS LOOK LIKE

Deal One

One of our Mentorship students, John, found a couple about to lose their home to foreclosure. After several conversations with this couple, he agreed to buy their house worth $175,000 for what was owed on it, plus the back payments. (The loan had an outstanding balance of $155,000, and back payments totaled $9,000.) He also agreed to give the seller $1,000 cash. He simply took over making the payments to the lender on the loan the sellers already had in place. Four years later, he still owns this property. To date, he has made more than $125,000 in appreciation from this property, plus he receives a cash flow of $250 a month from renting it out.

Deal Two

Michael, one of our students in New Orleans, found a motivated seller with a junker of a house. He put the property under contract to buy for $20,000. Its after-repair value was $60,000, but it needed about $15,000 worth of repairs. Not wanting to get involved with a rehab project (not to mention that he didn't have the $35,000 cash needed to buy and fix up the property himself), Michael sold his contract to another investor for $2,200 cash—his first of six deals during his first six months of investing.

Deal Three

Another student, Sally, bought a Department of Veterans Affairs (VA) foreclosure house and rehabbed the property. To fund the deal, Sally borrowed the money from her mother and agreed to pay it back at 9 percent interest when she resold the property. Sally kept the house as a rental for a while, paying her mom "interest only" payments every month and enjoying a positive cash flow because she had purchased the house so inexpensively. Last year, Sally resold the property and netted $35,000! In fact, Sally was so excited about this first deal that she "took to the bank" that she started a second one right away. She borrowed the needed $5,000 down payment from her credit union to pay to a seller in preforeclosure, then took over the payments on the seller's loan. As a result, she got $15,000 of equity and a positive cash flow from day one. She currently has more than $52,000 of equity in this one deal alone.

Deal Four

Gina, a full-time investor who read our book *Making Big Money Investing in Real Estate Without Tenants, Banks, or Rehab Projects* found a motivated seller who had moved from Colorado Springs, Colorado, to California because of a job change. The seller was about to lose his Colorado property to foreclosure when Gina helped him find a way out. The house was valued at $400,000 with two liens against it: a first mortgage of $351,000 and a second mortgage of $25,000. The seller wanted to save his credit from being ruined by a foreclosure; he knew he wouldn't get any money out of the sale. So Gina negotiated with the first mortgage holder to accept a "short sale" (discussed in Chapter 3) in the amount of $300,000 and the second mortgage holder to accept $8,000 as full payment for the money owed. This meant Gina was able to buy that $400,000 house for a total price of $308,000. Then she resold the house 30 days later for $360,000. After all closing costs, she netted $30,000. It was a win-win-win deal for everyone. The seller was thrilled to save his credit; the buyer was thrilled to save $40,000 on the purchase of his home; Gina was thrilled to make a healthy profit of $30,000.

Deal Five

Maggie, a Mentorship student from North Carolina, found a motivated seller who was about to lose a house she'd inherited from her mother due to foreclosure. Instead of fixing up the house and keeping it, Maggie sold her contract to another investor for $15,000 and gave $5,000 of that money to the seller. Thrilled with the outcome, the seller sent Maggie a note that read: *Thank you so very much. You've been a blessing to me. Before my mother died, she asked me not to lose her property. So this has been very painful for me. Thank you for helping me.*

Homeowners in foreclosure are going through a lot because they're dealing with the personal anguish of a very public failure. Add to this their possible feelings of shame, failure, and embarrassment, and you start to get the picture. They may also feel depressed and on the defensive. Some may simply be in denial, waiting for lottery winnings or a knight in shining armor to save the day. Many behave indecisively because they're confused about what's happening to them. So when you help sellers get out of tough places, you help them move on. You are providing a great service.

WHAT YOU CAN OFFER A HOMEOWNER FACING FORECLOSURE

As a knowledgeable investor, you can be of benefit to many of these homeowners by helping them with the following:

- Save their credit
- Salvage some or all of their equity
- End an embarrassing situation
- Release some of the worry and stress they feel
- Find them a fast solution to their foreclosure problem
- Decide what to do next, maybe even handling all of the details

DEFICIENCY JUDGMENTS

Many homeowners think that once the foreclosure sale is over, their worries end. This may not be true. In many states, the lender can get a *deficiency judgment* from the court. This means the borrower (homeowner) still owes the lender any money that the lender lost from the whole process. Many times, this pushes the homeowner to declare bankruptcy to escape this debt burden.

Because the law doesn't allow the lender to make a profit on a foreclosure, any moneys made at the foreclosure sale in excess of the amount owed the lender, including the foreclosure costs, go to the borrower. However, rarely does the borrower get anything for his or her equity in a foreclosure sale because the house is usually sold well below market price.

The lender can receive money for such fees as the following:

- Late penalties
- Accrued interest
- Attorney's fees
- Court costs
- Filing fees
- Title work fees

DEED OF TRUST VERSUS MORTGAGE

Each state has specific laws about how the foreclosure process operates in that state. One big distinction is whether your state uses a *deed of trust* to secure real estate loans or a *mortgage.*

While some states use both, all states use one or the other of these documents in the majority of loans. So find out if your state is a deed-of-trust state or a mortgage state by asking a local title company or real estate attorney which document is commonly used. You can also log on to your Bonus Web Pack, which includes a chart showing which type of state you are investing in. (For more information, see Appendix A.)

A deed of trust and a mortgage perform essentially the same role, namely, securing the lender's loan to a borrower. Let's explain some important differences.

A deed of trust is a three-party agreement involving the following players:

1. *Trustor:* The borrower
2. *Trustee:* A third party the bank chooses to look after the bank's interests
3. *Beneficiary:* The lender

When people borrow money in a deed-of-trust state, they sign a document (deed of trust) that gives legal title to the property to a trustee for the benefit of the lender (beneficiary). Now, the borrower really owns the property and has all kinds of rights to enjoy the property *up to a point.* The borrower cannot do anything that will jeopardize the lender's security in the house (like let it go into disrepair). Also, the borrower cannot stop paying the lender money owed without the trustee's foreclosing on the house.

In a deed-of-trust state, the process of foreclosure is also called a *nonjudicial foreclosure* because the foreclosure process doesn't take place in a courtroom in front of a judge; it happens through a *trustee's sale* of the property. The trustee must follow a specific set of rules established in each state. The final step is the sale of the property by auction run by the trustee for the benefit of the lender (beneficiary).

A mortgage, while used for essentially the same purpose, has some important differences. First, a mortgage is only a two-party agreement between the mortgagor (borrower) and mortgagee (lender).

With a mortgage, there is no third-party trustee to look after the lender's interest; the lender does this itself. When a mortgagor (the person who borrowed the money) defaults on the terms and conditions of the mortgage (the most important of which is to make timely payments to the lender as spelled out in the promissory note), the lender (mortgagee) proceeds with a *judicial foreclosure* on the property. It's called a judicial foreclosure because it takes place in a courtroom before a judge. Typically, a judicial foreclosure used in mortgage states takes longer than a trustee's sale.

Remember, each state has its own way of doing things, and you will need to research and learn the legal ropes in your area.

NONJUDICIAL FORECLOSURES (TRUSTEE'S SALES)

Here's how the foreclosure process for a nonjudicial or trustee's sale foreclosure works. It applies in states that use deeds of trust.

Step One: Borrower is Delinquent—
Preforeclosure Stage

The borrower misses a payment on his or her loan and, after the grace period, he or she falls delinquent on the loan. Because foreclosures are costly to lenders who prefer to collect payments rather than take back houses, most lenders will work with a homeowner for a period of 60 days to 90 days before they go to Step Two of the foreclosure process.

Step Two: Lender Files the Default—
Notice of Default Stage

At a certain point, the lender will no longer work with the borrower and will start the official legal process of foreclosing on the property. The lender files a notice of default (NOD) at the county recorder's office and mails a certified copy of the NOD to the borrower. In some states, the name of this document is different, but its purpose and function are the same. In Colorado, for example, the document that lenders use to record the default is called "notice of election and demand for sale by public trustee." That's just a long-winded way of saying it's an official notice that the foreclosure clock is ticking. (Note: In your Bonus Web Pack, we've

included a state-by-state listing of the exact process used by lenders to foreclose on the property. See Appendix A for details.)

During this stage, the borrower may reinstate the loan. This
means the borrower can make up the back payments and late
fees, bringing the loan back into good standing. If the borrower
does reinstate the loan, then the foreclosure stops. If the borrower
doesn't, the foreclosure process moves on to the next step.

Step Three: Lender Prepares to Force Sale of Property— Notice of Sale Stage

If the borrower doesn't bring the loan current during the
60 days to 90 days following the notice of default, the lender will
move ahead with plans to force the sale of the property. This sale
is called a trustee's sale because the trustee of the deed of trust
that the borrower signed conducts the auction.

In Step Three of the foreclosure process, the lender records
a notice of sale and advertises the pending foreclosure sale in a
general circulation newspaper for three to six weeks. In some
states, once the notice of sale (or the comparable document)
is recorded, the borrower can no longer reinstate the loan but
instead must pay off the outstanding balance. In other states, such
as California, the borrower has up to five business days before the
sale date to reinstate the loan. (See Appendix A for more details.)

Step Four: Trustee Conducts the Trustee's Sale— Public Auction

We finally reach the courthouse steps. The trustee auctions
the property off to the highest bidder, who must pay in cash or
certified funds. At this auction, the lender opens bidding with the
amount of money owed (including late fees and other foreclosure
costs), and if no one bids higher than that amount, the bank keeps
the property. If someone does bid higher, that person has a set

amount of time (usually a few hours or sometimes immediately) to produce the certified funds to purchase the property. Then the trustee executes a Trustee's Deed to the new owner.

Step Five: Buyer Waits for Redemption Period to Pass— Redemption Period

Not all states have a redemption period, but in those that do, the redemption period is the time after the foreclosure auction during which the borrower can pay the full amount of what was owed (the full balance of the loan including all fees and other foreclosure costs) to the trustee and get the property back. Meanwhile, the investor (or lender) who "purchased" the property at the auction has to wait out the redemption period. If the homeowner redeems the loan, the trustee refunds money paid to the lender/investor and returns the title to the property to the homeowner.

During this period, the homeowner usually lives in the house for free while determining where to move next. The lender or investor who "got" the house at auction can't harass or remove the homeowner until the redemption period has expired. (Note: In the rare case of the lender or investor showing a court that the homeowner is damaging the house and radically diminishing its value, that person may be able to get court permission to remove the homeowner.)

In most deed-of-trust states, the homeowner has *no* redemption rights, but this can vary. In some states, such as Colorado, the homeowner has a redemption period of 75 days. Almost all mortgage states have redemption periods.

JUDICIAL FORECLOSURES (USED IN MORTGAGE STATES)

Here's how the judicial foreclosure process goes in states that use mortgages.

Step One: Borrower Is Delinquent—
Preforeclosure Stage

The borrower misses a payment on the loan and, after the grace period ends, becomes delinquent on the loan. This step is the same in both a judicial and a nonjudicial foreclosure. The lender prefers not to foreclose but to have the borrower make timely payments.

Once the lender believes it's at risk of not getting the money, it quickly proceeds to Step Two—which *does* differ from the non-judicial process.

Step Two: Lender Files a Lawsuit—
Judicial Foreclosure Begins

The lender files an official document with the courts (a Complaint) that initiates the lawsuit to foreclose on the property. The lender also needs to give outside parties notice that the lawsuit is occurring by recording a *lis pendens* with the county recorder. This tells the world a "lawsuit pending" is on the property; therefore, anyone who has an interest in the property can take the appropriate steps to protect his or her interests. The borrower may answer the Complaint, which keeps the lender from getting a default judgment and slows down the process.

> **INSIDER SECRET:** One of the biggest challenges you face when investing in foreclosures is the increasing time pressure you must work under. One insider secret is to help the borrower file an answer to a lender's complaint. This sounds more complicated than it is. In reality, filing an answer is quick and easy, and it will delay the foreclosure process by up to a month. So just by helping your seller file this document, you gain up to 30 days to figure out how you'll purchase the property!

Step Three: Lender and Borrower Meet in Court

If the borrower has filed an answer with the court to the lender's complaint, then a court date is scheduled. That's when the judge will decide if the lender has the right to proceed with the foreclosure (the normal outcome of this hearing). If the court rules in the favor of the lender, it issues a judgment and sets a sale date.

Step Four: The Sheriff's Sale

Typically three weeks to four weeks after the sheriff's sale (functionally, the same thing as a trustee's sale) is advertised, the auction takes place, and the property is sold to the highest bidder. Once the sheriff's sale happens, a *certificate of sale* is issued to the buyer. In most states, the previous owner has the right to redeem (buy back) the property within a set period, sometimes as long as 12 months.

Step Five: Buying the House Back after the Sale— Redemption Period

The main difference in the redemption period in a judicial foreclosure is that almost all mortgage states *have* a redemption period. Also, the redemption period is typically longer in mortgage states than in deed-of-trust states—up to 12 months in some states. If the borrower doesn't redeem the property during this time, the new buyer gets title to the property through a document called a *sheriff's deed.*

INSIDER SECRET: In many states, the homeowner can *sell* his or her redemption rights to a third party—an investor like you! Imagine a case in which a house is auctioned and no one outbids the lender, but you *know* the house is worth significantly more. You connect with the owner and pay that person to assign his or her redemption rights to you. Then you use the redemption period to raise funds to pay the money owed to the lender (including the full loan balance, all costs, penalties, and accrued interest) and buy the house back. Sometimes the best deals can be made after the game appears to be over!

What happens to the homeowner after the foreclosure auction? It depends. If the borrower has any redemption rights (usually the case if the lender used a judicial foreclosure), then the new owner of the property must typically wait until the entire redemption period is over before getting the homeowner out of the property. If the property is rented, the new owner will require the tenants pay rent. After the borrower's redemption rights have expired or immediately after a trustee's sale (for nonjudicial foreclosure), the new owner files an eviction action—usually called an *unlawful detainer*—against the occupant. Unless the trustee made a serious mistake in the foreclosure process, the judge almost always sides with the new owner.

INSIDER SECRET: Many investors struggle with the idea of evicting people from their home, especially in a foreclosure situation. As you progress as an investor from Level One Investing through Level Three Investing (more on this in Chapter 9), you'll learn how to deal with difficult situations like this. Often, we pay the homeowner to move early rather than waiting out the process. It's called a *friendly eviction* because both you and the occupant agree on the terms of the early move. Be sure to put your agreement in writing and make sure you have possession of the house and the keys before you pay anything to the occupant.

BEST FORECLOSURE STAGE TO BUY IN

Which stage is best to buy in? While there are advantages to buying in each stage, our preference is to buy in the first one—preforeclosure—for three reasons:

1. *You have much less competition.* Because you've found most of these deals before other investors even know about them, you'll be able to negotiate one-to-one with the seller without other investors knocking at the door. This gives you the chance to negotiate a better deal. Remember, once a foreclosure officially starts, every investor in town knows about it and will be mailing, calling, or visiting the homeowner.

2. *You can get into investing with very little money.* When the foreclosure process is in the early stages, the homeowner tends to owe less money in back payments. Combine this fact with a simple yet powerful technique called *"subject to" financing* (see Chapter 3), and sellers may be willing to deed you the property in exchange for your making up the back payments and taking over the burden of the monthly payments. The seller gets a fast out and saves his or her credit, and you buy another investment property that often has a positive cash flow from day one (plus a chunk of equity). You also get to leverage your way into the deal without taking on the liability of personally guaranteeing any debt.

3. *You have plenty of time to find a solution.* Because the foreclosure hasn't technically started, you have at least a few months to close on the property and find an end buyer for the property (whether it's another investor to sell the deal to or one of the other exit strategies that you'll be learning about in this book).

Your second-best choice is to buy after the official notice but prior to the sale, that is, during the reinstatement period. In many states, even after the foreclosure has technically started, you can still make up the back payments and reinstate the loan. You bring the loan up-to-date and make payments every month as the seller did before getting behind. The major benefit to buying this way is that you can still use the existing financing as a way to leverage yourself into the deal. The downside is that once the official foreclosure has started, you'll encounter a lot more competition from other investors who now know about the seller's situation.

Your third-best choice is buying after the sale has occurred, either from the bank or by buying the seller's redemption rights. If you plan on being a cash buyer (and carefully read Chapter 3 before you decide you *can't* be a cash buyer), then buying directly from a bank might work well for you. Once a foreclosure auction takes place in which no one bids more than the bank, the property goes back to the bank and becomes a real estate owned (REO) property. It gets sold as quickly as possible by the lender. Remember, that lender is in the lending business, *not* in the housing business. Therefore, you can often get hefty discounts on these properties.

Also, once a property has been sold at auction, in many states, the seller still has the right to redeem the loan and buy back the property. As an investor, one strategy is to find a seller who's willing to sell you the redemption rights; then you buy back the property. This can be a highly profitable way to buy.

Ultimately, the biggest benefit of buying after the auction is that most investors think the game is over so you tend to have less competition. Also, the time crunch is less severe. This means you have more time to conduct your due diligence and have the property professionally inspected.

Your fourth-best choice is buying during the final days up to the actual sale date. While you can still make many profitable deals happen at this late stage, it's stressful and hurried, plus it often requires access to a lot of cash. The benefit of buying closer to the sale date is that many owners who have been in denial finally realize they *do need to act*. If you plan to buy at this stage, make sure you fully understand how to use the *short sale* technique described in Chapter 3.

■ Success Team—Peter's Story

One of our students, John, bought a house in an area of San Diego called Chula Vista. It was a three-bedroom, two-bath home in a nice area. The sellers were at the final stages of a foreclosure that they had dragged out as long as they could by declaring bankruptcy. He felt pressure to close fast, both from the sellers and from the lender. All along, he let the sellers know they would net about $25,000 after their share of all the closing costs. The sellers were happy with that; within a week, they left three voice-mail messages saying how grateful they were and how they understood that they would be getting around $25,000.

Well, the closing date came, and after all the costs were added up, the sellers ended up with a net check for $24,500. This was almost exactly the amount of money John had told them to expect. The next week, he got two messages from the sellers yelling at him at how unhappy they were with the money they received and how they were treated unfairly.

This was the first time I'd seen such an about-face from sellers. Since that time, I've seen it on other occasions when the seller was in the final stages of foreclosure. I've come to realize that it isn't about sellers being bad people; they're simply in an extremely stressful and scary place. Some people faced with these pressures don't react well, so they look for other people to lash out at. If you're going to buy during this stage of the foreclosure, be aware of this possibility and keep yourself emotionally whole. This took me quite a while to learn. ■

Our last choice is buying at the auction itself. While many experienced investors make great livings by buying properties at the actual foreclosure auctions, we tend to avoid purchasing at this stage for three reasons:

1. *It takes all cash to play this game!* This means no leverage unless you have a private investor backing you up.
2. *We believe it's the riskiest stage you can buy in because you won't be able to inspect the houses or take your time to conduct your due diligence.* When you combine this lack of due diligence with the need for an all-cash closing, you're taking a big risk unless you really know what you're doing.
3. *The auction process itself generally favors the selling party.* We've dealt with enough houses to know that you never want to be in a group of other buyers competing for the same house. This competition—combined with the natural human fear of losing a great deal—are two potent psychological factors working against you.

Here's one exception to buying at auction: if you're the only bidder, if you're experienced, and if you have checked out the house, then go ahead and bid on it. How can you be the only investor at the auction? Observe several auctions and get to know the regulars. Ask them which times and days tend to have the fewest competitors. Just in case they aren't willing to share that information, look for a property where the auction date was postponed. Other investors may miss the delayed auction so you might be the only one showing up to bid.

STUDY THE RULES

Our advice is to buy as early in the foreclosure process as possible because that's when you're likely to make the most money.

Those of us in the Mentor Family have profited in the tens of millions of dollars by buying distressed houses directly from the owners *before* the house is sold at auction. We believe this is the easiest entry point to start making money immediately by investing in foreclosures.

As an investor, you'll have to become familiar with the "rules" and the legal process of foreclosure in your state. (You can get a good start by checking out your state's laws in your Bonus Web Pack described in Appendix A.) Know what can stall a foreclosure process to give you, the investor, more time. For example, just filing an answer to the lender's complaint in some states can buy you an extra *month*. Or, for example in California, if the lender writes down the wrong information on the notice of default, you can force the lender to start all over with the paperwork, which can buy you as much as two to three months.

Remember, it's just a game. To get good at playing it, you've got to study the rules. Just as champion athletes have to put the effort in on the practice field, wealthy investors have to invest the time and energy to master the rules of the game. It's not glamorous, but it's the truth.

In the next chapter, you'll learn 12 specific strategies to structure moneymaking deals without your cash or credit.

3

12 WAYS TO STRUCTURE DEALS WITHOUT CASH OR CREDIT

How should you structure your offers to put together deals? You are about to learn the 12 best foreclosure buying strategies. Whether you are buying properties in foreclosure or in preforeclosure, these strategies will allow you to start making money right away.

If you read our book *Making Big Money Investing in Real Estate Without Tenants, Banks, or Rehab Projects,* you'll be familiar with a few of these buying strategies. But you'll notice that we have in this book completely left out any discussion of buying with a *lease option.* A lease option is when you lease out a property from a seller for a long period of time with an agreed-on option price at which you can buy the property at any point during the lease period. When buying foreclosures, a lease option is *not* the way you'll want to structure the deal. It's still a great way to buy homes in nice areas with nothing down; it's just not the best strategy to use with foreclosure deals. Rather, we want to share 12 other cutting-edge strategies, which have four factors in common.

FOUR FACTORS ESSENTIAL TO ANY SUCCESSFUL FORECLOSURE INVESTING SYSTEM

The four essential elements involved in successful foreclosure real estate investing are described below.

1. Little or No Money Down

You can make all these buying strategies work without putting a ton of your cash into the deals. For the buying strategies that do require cash, you'll learn how to minimize the amount of your money in the deal by tapping into insider sources to fund your deals. But if you do have capital to invest, you'll learn how to make safer decisions and stretch your investing dollars so you can build your portfolio even faster.

■ **Success Team—Peter's Story**

One of our students found an real estate owned (REO) property that a lender had taken back in a foreclosure. Using VA financing, our student was able to buy this $170,000 five-bedroom house for just $117,100 (including $6,800 of closing costs). After talking with her local bank manager, this student was able to get all the closing costs rolled into the loan, so she put nothing down. She then went out and sold the house for $159,000 in a quick sale. Not bad for a "zero-down" deal. ■

2. Find Funding, Even If Your Credit Is Bad

You can use all these buying strategies regardless of the condition of your credit. Some nontraditional funding sources for your deals couldn't care less if your credit has holes in it the size of Texas. You'll learn how to tap into specialized sources of financing that serious investors have been using for decades to make millions of dollars. (The ideas you'll learn have been called the "best-kept secrets of millionaire investors.")

■ **Success Team—Peter's Story**

Over the past 16 years, I've had my hand in hundreds of deals, and with the exception of only two properties, my credit has never been an issue. By that, I mean the seller or person I got the money from never ran a credit check. I know this sounds impossible, but when you use the ideas in this book, you'll realize that while good credit can help, it's *not* a requirement for making money investing in foreclosures. ■

3. Minimize Your Risk

Making money is important, but keeping the money you make is equally important. All of the foreclosure strategies in our system help you treat people right while you also isolate and minimize your risk.

■ **Success Team—Peter's Story**

One of the properties I bought years ago when I started investing was a two-bedroom condo that I purchased with conventional bank financing with a healthy chunk of my own money as a down payment and a personal guarantee on the loan. A tenant who had some unsavory friends was living in my unit. The police came and knocked on my tenant's door to talk with these "friends," who broke the back window and jumped out the second-story window to run for it. Looking back, I still remember how much emotional stress that tenant caused me.

Fast-forward to a deal I did using the system you are learning. I have an investment property in Colorado Springs that was vacant for two months. Because I had none of my money in the deal and no personal guarantee on the financing, I didn't feel anywhere near the same amount of stress as I'd felt in the past. I simply fired the property management company and found someone else to take over and fill the vacancy. It felt like a Monopoly game—as if I were losing a little money in a game rather than the highly personal feeling of having my hard-earned cash at risk on the condo. That's the way I like to do my investing now—to risk potentially some of my profit, but never have my capital or credit at stake. ■

4. Help Sellers Win

You will be working with sellers who need your help. When you buy a foreclosure property the right way, you create a win-win transaction that helps sellers effectively deal with tough personal situations.

■ **Mentor Family—Coach John's Story**
I purchased a three-bedroom house in San Diego on which the sellers were five payments behind on their mortgage. The husband was fairly ill, and I remember going back to the house after we had signed the contract and talking with his wife. After a few minutes, she asked me into the bedroom because her husband wanted to see me. As we walked in and I saw the husband stretched out in the bed, I felt awkward. But then he started to thank me for helping them make the best of a bad situation. He was having serious back problems and couldn't work. They were about to lose the house when I offered to help them with a better way out. I left that day knowing I'd made a difference as an investor. ■

TRADITIONAL WAYS TO BUY FORECLOSURES

Before explaining the buying strategies that are essential to our system, let's look at how most people invest in foreclosures so you can see the benefits of using the foreclosure strategies described in this book.

Traditionally, most investors buying foreclosures seek houses they can get good prices on (either directly with the owner, through a real estate agent, at an auction, or directly from the bank) for an *all-cash* closing. This means either the investors take the money out of their personal bank accounts or borrow from a traditional lender. Truth be told, this is a good way to invest, and these investors make lots of money. But the majority of people who want to start investing find themselves excluded because they don't have the cash or credit to do these deals the traditional way.

Also, while these traditional investors make money, in many cases they take on magnitudes of risk—risk they easily could avoid by using the strategies you are about to learn.

Let's be clear—any way you structure a deal that allows you to purchase a foreclosure and make a profit in a win-win way is fine by us. Even if you simply want to use our ideas to fine-tune your traditional foreclosure investing, this book gives you the tools and techniques to do this. If you're looking for more than that—if you want buying strategies that are simple yet powerful enough that they work regardless of the quality of your credit or the size of your bank account—you'll find these ideas will supercharge your investing profits.

 ■ **Success Team—Peter's Story**

It surprises many beginning investors when I recommend that, even if they do have money or great credit, they get started investing *without* using their own cash or conventional bank loans. They find it hard to believe that sometimes having money can be detrimental to learning to be the best investor you can be. I've seen money used as a crutch to make a marginal deal go through. I admit I've been guilty of getting lazy and throwing money into a deal where a little more imagination and prudent negotiation would have served me better. But with an open mind and the right education, not having money can push you to be a faster, more creative, and more skilled investor.

What's more, you'd be surprised how fast you can pour your liquid cash reserves into real estate. I've watched traditional investors pour more than $1 million into several deals in a matter of months and then have to wait until they sold those properties before they could free up enough of their money to go out and buy more properties. You'll never regret learning to buy without money. It will make you a much more savvy investor for those times you *do* decide to use your own money or conventional financing. ∎

THE FOUNDATIONAL FORECLOSURE BUYING STRATEGY

If you are just getting started investing, structuring deals with sellers in foreclosure can seem overwhelming as you try to remember the various ways of conducting them. If you are locked into using only one buying strategy with sellers in foreclosure, however, the one we recommend is buying properties "subject to" the seller's loan. It's that powerful.

If you read *Making Big Money Investing in Real Estate Without Banks, Tenants, or Rehab Projects*, you already know we often use a lease option as the foundational technique when buying investment properties from motivated sellers who *aren't* in foreclosure. This buying strategy, referred to as a *"subject to"* technique, is the foundational buying strategy for working with homeowners who *are* in foreclosure.

When beginner Mentorship students come through our workshops, they struggle with information overload. It can be compared to a new mechanic who is given a toolbox with an overwhelming number of unfamiliar and specialized tools. That's why we highly encourage you to master one or two tools first. Once you get comfortable using those tools, then layer in another tool, then another, and another.

As you read through this chapter with all its buying strategies, you don't need to "get" them all on the first go-round. Lock onto one or two buying strategies that you can put to work making you money, then add in other layers of strategies later. If you have too many options at once, you run the risk of freezing up when meeting with a seller.

Imagine you are meeting with a motivated seller in the early stages of foreclosure and that seller owns a well-kept house in an area you like. You sit down with this owner, and after you've spent time getting to know her situation thoroughly, she says, "I just want out. I don't care about the equity. I just want to walk away from the house. I'm at the end of my rope, and if you don't want to buy it for what I owe, then I'll just let the bank come and take it."

You see the seller looking right at you and know all she wants is to stop this foreclosure that's draining all her energy. The house is worth $200,000. With $4,000 worth of paint and carpeting, it would probably be worth $225,000. She owes $190,000 as a first mortgage with monthly payments of principal, interest, real estate taxes, and insurance (PITI) totaling $1,350 (see Figure 3.1).

FIGURE 3.1 *Assessing the Costs*

After-repair value of house	$225,000
Current "as is" value of house	$200,000
Needed repairs (paint, carpet, etc.)	$4,000
Existing first mortgage	$190,000
PITI payments on first mortgage	$1,350
Back payments owed	$4,000

She's got two real problems. First, she's behind three months in her payments. With late fees, that comes to more than $4,000— money she simply doesn't have. Second, even if she could find a way to make up the back payments, she still has no way of scraping together $1,350 each month after that. More than anything, she just wants you to take the house for what she owes and she'll go find a place to rent for $800 a month, which is all she can really afford.

Many investors would look at this situation and calculate whether it makes sense to take $200,000 cash to buy a house worth $225,000. (The $200,000 cash is the total cost of the property after paying off the $190,000 loan, plus the $4,050 of back payments, plus $4,000 of cosmetic work, plus $2,000 of closing costs.) But if you were a cash buyer, this deal wouldn't work for you because that $25,000 of equity would get eaten up quickly with holding costs, plus the closing costs of the second closing once you resold the house.

Some investors might go ahead and buy it anyway with the intention of holding the house as a long-term rental. Fair enough, but it really wasn't much of a bargain for a cash purchase.

Other investors would try to get that $200,000 (or a large chunk of it) by borrowing it from a conventional lender. While this would be a way to leverage your way into the deal, it comes with the following three main disadvantages:

1. *The cost of the money.* After adding up all the costs of getting that new loan, you would have eaten up around $5,000 of your equity. Following are some of those costs that make your banker, not you, rich:
   - Loan origination fee
   - Prepaid interest or "points"
   - Credit check fee
   - Property appraisal
   - Document delivery fees
   - Recording fees

2. *Your lender will require that you sign personally on the loan.* That means if anything goes wrong with the house or the housing market in your area, regardless of whose fault it is, your credit (and potentially other assets) are on the line.

3. *You'll have to jump through the hoops of qualifying for traditional financing.* The lender will want to review credit checks, long loan applications, bank statements, and tax returns. And just when you thought it had everything, your lender almost always finds two or three more things. Are you told about all this up front? No! The lender waits until the week before you're supposed to close. So you spend the last week before closing scrambling to make the deal work. (Notice that we're just a bit jaded about this.)

Who needs all that stress? Wouldn't it be better to step in and take over making payments on the seller's loan? You can do this once you have the specialized knowledge you are about to learn.

THE BEST-KEPT SECRET IN REAL ESTATE—BUYING "SUBJECT TO" THE EXISTING FINANCING

Over the years, thousands of investors across the country have asked us to mentor them to become financially free. If you were one of our Mentorship students and brought this deal to us to discuss, here's how we'd coach you through it:

You: The seller just wants to walk away from the house and doesn't want anything for her equity. I know there is a deal here. Help!

Mentor: OK, let's take this step-by-step. Tell me about her motivation to sell.

You: She was living with her boyfriend who was helping to make the payment each month. But six months ago they split up. She struggled to make the payments for a few months, then she just couldn't do it anymore. She's three payments behind now, and you have all the other financial details I submitted through the Mentorship Students' website. She said if I don't buy it, she'll let it go back to the bank.

Mentor: Do you remember from the home study materials about the strategy of buying "subject to" the existing financing?

You: I remember some of it.

Mentor: Tell me what you remember because this is how I'm going to coach you to buy this house. The best part is that you'll be able to do it with nothing down and very little risk.

You: Well, it means I buy the property but don't pay off her loan. I just have her deed me the property and make up her back payments, then each month I just send in the payment to her lender. Is that right?

Mentor: Yes. She deeds you the house for a token payment up front. Usually, we'll use $10. Strange as it seems, for this to be legally binding, you need to pay something. It's called *consideration,* which is just a fancy legal term that means you gave her something of value to make the contract binding. You then clean up the property and start marketing it. Chances are, you'll be able to sell the house either on a rent-to-own basis or on an owner-carry (see Chapter 8) and collect $8,000 to $20,000 up front, depending on which of the exit strategies you use. Then using your new buyer's money, you'll send in the back payments to the lender along with a letter explaining this is to bring this specific loan current. Each month after that, you'll send in the payment to her lender with the loan number on the check.

TOP FIVE BENEFITS OF BUYING "SUBJECT TO" FINANCING

Following are the five top benefits of the "subject to" existing financing buying process:

1. You'll make money up front from your buyer, which you'll use to bring the loan current and pay yourself back for the minor fix-up you did.
2. You'll create a monthly cash flow.
3. You'll get all the tax benefits because you'll own the property.
4. You'll earn extra profit as the principal balance on the loan pays down each month (*amortization*).
5. You'll get a big check on the back end of the deal when your buyer or tenant-buyer cashes you out.

Going back into our coaching session . . .

You: Can I really do this? It sounds too good to be true. Is this legal?

Mentor: That's a common question. The answer is "Yes, this is a perfectly legitimate way to buy property." For years, savvy investors have been using this method to buy properties intelligently and make a lot of money doing it. In fact, I've used this buying strategy myself on more than 100 houses over the past 11 years, and it's made me wealthy. Still, there are risks you need to be aware of—you must look out for yourself in the deal.

You: I've heard there's something called a due-on-sale clause, which means if I bought the house like this, then the lender would call the loan "due in full."

Mentor: That's right. The lender has the right granted in the deed of trust or mortgage securing this loan to call it due in full if the house is sold without getting cashed out. But the due-on-sale clause, which is the biggest reason investors are leery of using this buying strategy, is really a paper tiger.

DUE-ON-SALE CLAUSE NOT A BIG PROBLEM

Just about every loan written for the past 20 years to 30 years contains a due-on-sale clause. According to this clause, if a borrower sells the property without paying off the loan, the lender has the right to accelerate that loan and call it due in full within 30 days.

Here's what the technical language typically sounds like:

> *If title to the property described herein, or any interest therein, is transferred without the Lender's prior written permission, the Lender may declare all sums secured by this agreement immediately due and payable.*

Sounds tough, doesn't it? But the due-on-sale clause is more intimidation than substance. Banks don't like borrowers to sell without the new borrower is *assuming* the loan (and paying points, loan fees, etc.) or obtaining a new loan (paying loan costs, potentially higher interest, and starting the amortization of the loan from scratch!).

Interestingly enough, *Black's Law Dictionary* defines a *due-on-sale clause* as a "device for preventing the subsequent purchasers from assuming loans with lower than market interest rates." However, would a bank call a 15 percent loan due when the current market rates were 8 percent? Probably not. But if the loan is at 8 percent and the market rate is 15 percent, you can bet your local lender would just love to call the loan due to force you to refinance the property at a higher interest rate. (The banker figures that even if you refinance the property with a different bank, at least you would have to cash out its old loan, giving it more money to lend at a higher interest rate.)

But banks are not in business to accelerate loans unless either you flaunt it (i.e., you dare them to call the loan due because you bought the house without paying off the loan) or interest rates have jumped dramatically.

■ **Success Team—Coach Robb's Story**

I've seen a lot of investors miss out on huge profits because they just don't understand how far banks will go *not* to foreclose on a property. Banks don't want to own real estate, and they don't want to have bad loans on their books. They simply want people to pay them on time and take care of the house. When you understand this, you recognize how much power you have when negotiating with lenders to find creative solutions to help sellers solve their problems. The key is to *communicate* with the lender about what you need to make this work for its best interest, which is to have the loan brought current.

Many times, I have a three-way call involving me, the seller, and the lender. The seller introduces me to the lender as "a friend who knows more about this real estate thing than I do and who is helping me understand what exactly is going on and how I can make sure you get your money."

Then I take over and find out the specific details and exact status of the loan. Many times, I negotiate a payment plan known as a forbearance agreement with the lender right there on the phone.   ■

NEGOTIATING A FORBEARANCE AGREEMENT

While talking with the lender before buying the property "subject to" the existing financing, it's best to work out a payment plan that helps you spread out the amount of money owed in back payments over time or, even better, adds the back payments onto the principal balance of the loan. This payment plan or workout is known as a *forbearance agreement.*

Remember, because this payment plan can be the critical piece you need to buy the property, you're negotiating with the lender on the seller's behalf and not as a new investor looking to buy the property. Getting the seller's permission to do this is easy. You can hold a three-way phone conversation with the lender or get written permission from the seller to allow the lender to discuss the matter with you.

From the lender's point of view, there are two main issues to work through:

1. How soon you can start making the current and future monthly payments
2. How you propose to pay the past-due amount (the payments in arrears)

In general, most lenders are more concerned with the monthly payments starting up and with the stability of these future payments than with when the past-due amount will be paid. As a creative investor, you have lots of options. For example, you could negotiate to do the following:

- Start making monthly payments now, delay for three months or six months the other money owed (arrears), then make it up in one or several payments.
- Pay the arrears over time (3, 6, 12, or 18 months) while making the monthly payment from here on.
- Get a moratorium on any payments for several months (explaining to the lender why the seller needs this time and why things will be securely different at that future date).
- Add the arrears to the principal balance and start immediately to make the monthly payments. (This is sometimes

called *recasting* the loan—adding the back payments to the loan and restarting it.)

- Make up the back payments in one payment with monthly payments to begin in 30 days.
- Make sure you get the lender to acknowledge in writing any agreement for a workout plan. Never rely on an oral agreement. And don't send money to the lender until you have conducted all your due diligence (see Chapter 6).

YOU'VE BOUGHT THE PROPERTY "SUBJECT TO" THE EXISTING FINANCING—NOW WHAT?

One of the best parts of buying a house "subject to" the existing financing is that it opens up so many options for your exit strategies for the property. (We'll be going into detail on different exit strategies in Chapter 7 and Chapter 8.)

Some of your exit strategies are as follows:

- Hold and rent it
- Immediately resell the property to a retail buyer
- Wholesale the house to another investor
- Rehab and resell the house to a retail buyer
- Sell on a rent-to-own basis
- Sell on a wraparound mortgage or land contract

 ■ **Success Team—Peter's Story**

One of the real estate agents I work with met a motivated seller at a baseball card show. The seller was one payment behind on his mortgage on a four-unit building. I agreed to pay the seller $119,000, of which 3 percent was in cash to cover my agent's commission and the balance was me taking over the property "subject to" the seller's existing first and second mortgages. I also agreed to make up the month's back payment on the first and second mortgages and to make payments on them each month thereafter. I kept the building as a rental and four years later sold it for an $80,000 profit.   ■

THREE BIGGEST QUESTIONS ABOUT BUYING "SUBJECT TO" THE EXISTING FINANCING

Following are three serious questions often asked about real estate transactions "subject to" the existing financing:

1. *How will the seller get a new loan if this loan stays in her name and appears on her credit record?* This can be a potential sticking point with a seller. But most lenders will credit the seller with having made the full payment as long as you can show them proof the loan has been paid for more than12 months (e.g., canceled checks, etc.) and that the property has been sold (copy of the purchase agreement).

   In some cases, the new lender won't give a 100 percent credit for the payments but rather only a 75 percent to 80 percent credit, just as if the property were being rented out on a long-term basis. In this case, it may have some effect on the seller getting a new loan. As long as the seller has the income to make up for this and his income-to-debt ratios are in line with the lender's requirements, this won't be a problem.

   Also, most people you buy from using this strategy are in foreclosure for a reason—they can't make the payments. Their need to solve this problem is a hundredfold more important to them than getting another loan down the road. Besides, if they lose the house to foreclosure, they'll have an even tougher time getting a loan later on because their credit will be trashed. This way, you save the seller's credit by bringing the loan current and making timely payments each month after that. In fact, every monthly payment you make improves the seller's credit history!

2. *Who gets the tax write-offs?* The person whose name is on the title gets the tax write-offs. That is you, the investor, gets the write-offs. Or if you resold the property on either a land contract or wraparound mortgage, then your buyer would get the tax write-offs.

3. *What if the seller doesn't want her name on the loan forever?* Negotiate for the longest time possible, then use a clause such as the following in your purchase contract:

> *Buyer agrees to pay off the Seller's loan(s) described above in this agreement within _____ months of closing of title. This clause shall survive the closing of title.*

■ Success Team—Coach Juli's Story

Learning and applying this one technique can dramatically change your life. I recently heard from Rodney, a Mentor Program student. He wrote, "Here's an update on a deal I found on a bandit sign. The homeowner was a divorcée whose husband had been living in the house. He had decided to abandon the property and move to Las Vegas in a month. The seller didn't want her credit to be affected by this sale. The house was such a mess, she was embarrassed to have me look at it. She thought it might sell for $110,000 once it was fixed up. She was not in a position to cover the payments or do any of the fix-up work herself.

I bought it with no money down, using your system to leave the existing financing in place. The loan amount was $90,000 and PITI was $750. My up-front costs included $2,000 in cash, a $1,000 promissory note, and $1,500 to replace the flooring (the tenants completed the installation).

I'm renting the house for $850, with a 5 percent increase each year. The tenants have a three-year option to purchase the property for $140,000. Other than the flooring, I spent no money on repairs, just took the junk out of the house and hauled it to the dump. My mortgage on the house is $90,000. My up-front payment was $4,500. If the tenants exercise their purchase option of $140,000, my profit from equity will be $45,500.

> Cash flow = $3,000 up-front payments + $100/month for
> 3 years = $3,600 = $6,600

That means the total profit will be approximately $52,100.

If these tenants don't buy, I will have an improved property that will sell for $150,000 with a real estate agent. There is no balloon on this "subject to" the financing deal. I now have a home in a good neighborhood that is appreciating well.   ■

SHORT-TERM "SUBJECT TO" EXISTING FINANCING WHEN REHABBING

As you may know from reading *Making Big Money Investing in Real Estate Without Tenants, Banks, or Rehab Projects*, we're not big on recommending rehab projects. Here's why. We see people start investing with the idea to buy an ugly house, fix it up, then resell it. But invariably they forget to factor in the *real* costs involved with a rehab project—financial, time, and emotional costs.

The Real Costs of a Rehab Project

Rehabbing real estate can be costly in the following three ways:

1. *The financial cost.* Most investors do factor in this cost up front. However, many find that once they start doing the work, hidden repairs eat into their profits.
2. *The time cost.* It's easy to forget to factor in the intense month or two of work to get the house rehabbed and back on the

market. This is especially important if you do some or all of the work yourself, rather than hiring outside contractors. Make sure the profit in the deal is worth all your time and energy.

3. *The emotional cost.* This is the cost most investors fail to calculate. Having thousands of dollars at stake for a two-month or three-month period can create stress, especially if you don't have the financial cushion to cover additional rehab costs or a slow resale market.

A Smarter Way to Fund a Rehab

If you do plan to buy foreclosures, rehab, and then sell them at retail prices, here is a better way to structure your deals. If you use this strategy, you will limit your risks and lower the amount of up-front money you put into the deal.

Imagine you find a seller who has a dumpy house in a nice part of town. The house needs serious repairs—about $30,000 worth—but once they're complete, the house will be worth $330,000. The seller is four months behind on the $210,000 first mortgage, which has monthly payments of $1,800, and agrees to sell you the house for $230,000.

You could put 20 percent down ($46,000) and get a loan for the remaining $184,000. In this case, you'd still need $30,000 cash for the repairs. If you did this, you'd net around $36,000. This would give you a return on investment (ROI) on your $83,500 of 43 percent—not bad, especially when you consider you made that return over three or four months (see Figure 3.2).

However, we suggest you buy the house for a price of $230,000 "subject to" the seller's first mortgage of $210,000. You'd then immediately make up the $8,000 of back payments to reinstate the loan and get started on the $30,000 worth of repairs. You'd agree to give the seller his or her money out of your profits when you resell the newly rehabbed house to a retail buyer.

The seller wins because he or she not only stops the foreclosure but also receives money within 90 to 120 days. (Notice that we switched to 90 to 120 days instead of three to four months. The change in terms makes the seller feel as though his or her cash comes faster—in days not months.)

We call this strategy of structuring the deal a *short-term "subject to" rehab*. Its main benefit is that it allows you to reduce the cash you need up front to approximately $45,000. This is not only $38,500 less cash needed up front—pushing your ROI to 88 percent—but it means you won't need to get bank financing for the other $184,000 to make this deal work! (See Figure 3.3.)

FIGURE 3.2 *Traditional Way to Fund a Rehab*

After-repair value (ARV) of house	$330,000
Your price	$230,000
Needed repairs	($30,000)
Closing costs (when buying)	($2,500)
Loan costs	($4,000)
Holding costs	($5,000)
Closing costs (when selling)	($2,500)
REALTOR® commission (when selling)	($20,000)
Net profit	**$36,000**
Down payment	$46,000
Closing costs (buying)	$2,500
Holding costs	$5,000
Repair costs	$30,000
Total cash invested	**$83,500**

Net profit ÷ cash invested = ROI
$36,000 ÷ $83,500 = 43% ROI (in a 3-month to 4-month period)

FIGURE 3.3 *A Better Way to Fund Your Rehab—Short-Term "Subject to" Financing*

After-repair value (ARV) of house	$330,000
Your price	$230,000
Existing first mortgage taking "subject to"	($210,000)
Needed repairs	($30,000)
Closing costs (when buying)	($2,500)
Holding costs	($5,000)
Closing costs (when selling)	($2,500)
Realtor commission (when selling)	($20,000)
Net profit	**$40,000**
Back payments made up on seller's existing mortgage	$8,000
Closing costs (when buying)	$2,500
Holding costs	$5,000
Repair costs	$30,000
Total cash invested	**$45,500**

Net profit ÷ cash invested = ROI
$40,000 ÷ $45,500 = 88% ROI (in a 90- to 120-day period)

This saves you many hours of getting your loan application and paperwork together and dramatically lowers your risk in this deal. It also saves you about $4,000 in loan costs for the money you'd have had to borrow if you didn't buy the house "subject to" the existing financing.

■ **Success Team—Peter's Story**

One of the first foreclosure deals I ever did was a junker of a house I bought for $9,500 "subject to" the seller's financing. I didn't make a ton of money on it, but I still have a photograph of the house on the wall of my office. Why? Because after buying this house, I really *felt* like an investor. ■

WHOLESALING OR "FLIPPING" DEALS FOR QUICK CASH PROFITS

In the world of real estate investing, if a deal doesn't fit what the investor is looking for, then it's usually passed by. Once you understand how to keep your radar screen open to finding deals that don't fit your investing strategy but that you can wholesale to other investors, you'll make thousands of dollars more each and every year.

Most investors look only for deals that fit into their limited view of how they buy and sell properties. For example, if an investor buys foreclosures that need fixing up and then resells these properties to a retail buyer, he or she develops tunnel vision in the search for this type of deal. This tunnel vision can result in completely missing out on the chance to buy a foreclosure "subject to" existing financing or turning the property into a long-term rental. This can be costly because for every single deal that meets this one-track investor's criteria, five other deals slip by. This investor loses potential profits forever, simply from not being open to other approaches.

While it's important to create a niche with your investing and develop a cookie-cutter process you can repeat within this niche, we also know the most successful investors profit from the deals they spot, even if these deals aren't ones they keep for themselves.

❝ ■ Success Team—Angela's Story

Seeing our clients grow amazes me. Nowhere is this more apparent than in watching our Mentorship Program coaches. They started as students themselves, but they are now full-time investors and part-time coaches helping our clients further their investment careers.

Emily is a great example of this. She is amazing at capturing every detail about how she takes a deal all the way to the bank. In addition, she takes great pride in walking others step-by-step through the process. Emily found a property she wanted to flip while driving through a neighborhood on the way home from an appointment. There had been a fire, and the house had a small For Sale sign on it with an out-of-area phone number. Emily called and, before long, negotiated a purchase price of $7,500 with $200 in earnest money. By the time she closed on the house, she had found a buyer willing to pay $15,000 for the property with $1,000 earnest money. When the buyer's earnest money check bounced, Emily called a back-up buyer who had offered her $10,000 cash for the property. She had a simultaneous closing the next day, and she netted just over $2,000 after paying the closing costs for the attorney.

The whole deal took about three weeks from finding it to closing with the buyer and seller. Here's the voice-mail message Emily recorded for would-be buyers who called about the property:

> *Hi, thanks for calling. If you're a rehabber who likes serious construction projects, you're in luck. The property you're calling about in the Greenville area is a three-bedroom, one-bath home with a laundry room. Similar homes in good shape sell for $80,000 to $90,000. If you act quickly, you can buy this one for just $15,000.*
>
> *What's wrong with the property? Well, a lot. There was a fire in the unfinished basement, and the fire charred the floor joists for the main level. The floor joists would need to be replaced or reinforced. The upstairs sustained extensive smoke damage. There are broken windows and a hole in the roof made by the firefighters. I'm not a construction expert—that's why I'm selling the property—but I imagine if you took it back to the framing and replaced the drywall, carpet, bathroom, and kitchen, you'd be off to a good start. The electrical system and HVAC will also need to be replaced along with the siding.*

Scraping off the house and rebuilding on the foundation is also a possibility. At this low price, you could spend $40,000 to $50,000 on completely new construction and still make money.

If you're up for the job of fixing up this house and making a huge profit on it, go out and take a look, then give me a call when you're ready to buy. There is a lockbox on the door, and bring a flashlight with you because the windows are boarded up. The address is ＿＿＿＿＿＿＿＿＿＿＿＿ .

Here's the ad Emily ran:

Handyman Special
Cash, Cheap. Lockbox. 3 bedrooms.
Fire Damage. Worth $80K fixed up. Will sell for $15K.

Imagine you were just starting out in the fishing industry. You bought a boat and spend your days putting out your nets and hauling in tuna. But one day when you come back into port, you notice that the boat docked next to you is selling a type of fish you've never seen before. The captain says that it's called yellowfish and that, while he never understood why people liked it, he'd found a few local restaurants that bought these fish at a healthy profit. In fact, he tells you he doesn't even specialize in catching yellowfish; they just end up in his nets while he's looking for tuna.

Over the next few weeks, you notice you've been hauling in many of these yellowfish while fishing for tuna. You think: rather than throwing these fish back into the ocean (what you have been doing since you got started), why not sell them to local restaurants too. So that day, you put the yellowfish you catch into a separate cooler.

When you get back to shore, you talk with four local restaurant owners who agree to buy your catch. You're amazed at how easy it was. In fact, you made such good money with such little extra effort that you start to cultivate relationships with more restaurants so you'll always have ready buyers for these yellowfish.

You can do exactly the same thing in your foreclosure investing. It's called *wholesaling* or *flipping deals*—when you take a deal you've contracted for with a seller and sell your rights under that contract to a third party. This third party, often another investor, pays you a cash fee to assign your interest under that contract over to him or her. The third party then buys the house from the seller. It's like taking the yellowfish you didn't want and selling them to another person for a quick cash profit.

Just like the fisherman looking for tuna, you might be looking primarily for sellers in preforeclosure who will let you make up a few months' back payments and deed you the house "subject to" their existing financing. Your plan calls for you to hold on to these houses for 10 years or more. But you keep coming across sellers in foreclosure who want to dump their houses. They aren't willing to sell their homes to you "subject to," but they have lots of equity and are willing to give you a great cash price. You see that these houses (the yellowfish) will need a big rehab effort, and you aren't interested in doing the work. But, still, you paid for the marketing that got these sellers to call you, and you invested your time to meet with them, so you decide to flip these deals. You negotiate the best deals you can, then find other investors to buy the deals from you for a cash fee.

■ Mentor Family—Byron's Story

Here's an example of a wholesale deal that Byron, one of the students in our Mentorship Program, did. He found a seller who owned a fourplex that needed some cosmetic fixing. The seller, a referral from another seller Byron had worked with, was five payments behind and headed for foreclosure. Although Byron met with the seller and locked up a great deal, he didn't want to keep it for himself, doing the repairs and managing the fourplex.

Instead, he sold his rights under the purchase contract to another investor for an assignment fee of $15,000.

The seller got a fair solution that included stopping the foreclosure and making $13,000 when the investor closed on the house. The investor who bought the deal got a great price and terms on a solid rental property in an area where he was already building his portfolio. And Byron made $15,000 for five hours of time invested. It was a win-win-win transaction. ■

So the next time you find a deal that doesn't meet your buying criteria, negotiate the best deal you can (whether for a cash sale or a "subject to" deal or some other strategy) and sign it up. Even if you don't want to keep the deal, try to flip it to a third party for a fast cash profit. (See Chapter 7 for details on how to flip properties.)

■ Success Team—Peter's Story

I picked up a contract on a house in need of a total rehab. I looked at all that necessary work and said, "There's no way I'm going to spend the next two months fixing it up." So I sold my contract for $1,500. All total, I spent less than 10 hours of my time on the deal. That meant I earned more than $150 an hour. Considering I was still working as an auto mechanic for a lot less money at the time, that money helped me change my self-image. I could see my time being worth so much more than I was getting trading dollars for hours in the garage. ■

INSIDER SECRET: Many of our Mentorship students focus on one strategy, such as lease options or buying homes "subject to" existing financing. Stephen and his wife, Susan, are a good example of this. After completing the Mentorship

Program, they bought several homes using lease options. They moved into Level Two Investing using the "subject to" financing strategy and buying 26 homes. Still eager for greater challenges, they made the jump to Level Three Investing. As Commercial Mentoring students, they have purchased more than 72 apartment units and are currently running 5 land development projects. Stephen and Susan have all kinds of units—duplex, threeplex, fourplex, a 13-unit, a 20-unit, and 11 condos. They stopped adding to their multiunits 18 months ago when they began doing Level Three development. Flipping foreclosures to other investors has been critical to their success. It gave them the cash flow to live on while they waited for the long-term profits to "ripen" from some of their other deals.

SHORT SALES: MAKING BIG MONEY ON HOUSES WITH LITTLE OR NO EQUITY

When you are investing in foreclosures, you'll likely run into sellers who have little or no equity in their properties. You might think that if they have no equity, you can't help them. In fact, when most investors look at a deal in which the property has no equity and the existing financing payments are too high to cover by putting a tenant into the property (which rules out buying "subject to" the existing financing), they pass on the deal because they don't see any way to structure it and still make a conservative profit for their time, effort, and risk.

But there is a way—called a *short sale*—that lets you take many of these no-equity deals and turn a fair, fast, and healthy profit on them. In a short sale, you negotiate with lenders to take less than what they're owed as full payment on a loan. For example, a lender has a $200,000 first mortgage on a house in foreclosure and is willing to accept $147,000 as full payment on the loan.

Why would lenders take less than they're owed? It's because of all the *real* costs they face when they're forced to foreclose on a property. First, a lender may lose money when it forecloses on a house. Foreclosure costs include attorney's fees, staff time, court or legal process fees, plus the huge discounts for auctioned properties.

Next, a lender may know the house's condition has severely deteriorated since the time it made the original loan, so the property may be financed over the "as is" value.

Finally, lenders face strict federal regulations regarding the ratio of bad loans they have on their books and the amount of money that must be kept in liquid reserves to balance this. With all these painful consequences of having to foreclose, it's no surprise that many lenders are willing to take a short sale to solve quickly an otherwise drawn-out process.

■ **Success Team—Commercial Coach Rob's Story**

Laura, one of our Mentorship students, received a call from a motivated seller in response to a postcard and flyer she had mailed him. The seller had spent $15,000 rehabbing the house, which he did all wrong. Then his wife got laid off from her job, and they were losing the house to foreclosure. The house was worth $120,000 and had two mortgages on it—a first for $75,000 and a second for $8,000. The seller agreed to sell it to Laura for $50,000, provided she could get his two lenders to accept a short sale in that total amount. She contacted the lenders and sent them the ugly photos of the property, her repair list and bids, the low comps for the house, and the seller's financial information. They had their real estate agent come out and do a broker's price opinion (BPO).

When the negotiations with the lenders were over, the first mortgage holder accepted a short sale in the amount of $49,000, and the second mortgage holder accepted a short sale in the amount of $5,000. Both lenders made their acceptance of her short sale offer contingent on Laura's getting them their money within 21 days. She immediately got on the phone to three private lenders she worked with and borrowed the money to buy the property and make the needed repairs. Laura refinanced the property and pulled $20,000 out of it. She currently has the house on the market to sell on a rent-to-own basis for $140,000.   ■

Best Situations for Short Sales

Here is a list of the most common situations in which short sales are appropriate. Note that the loan(s) *must* be in default or the lender(s) will not accept a short sale.

- The property in foreclosure is financed so high that the lender stands to lose a significant amount of money if the house goes to auction.
- The physical condition of the property has deteriorated so badly that only an investor would buy it at an auction and command a steep discount in price before bidding on it.
- A large second mortgage is at risk because the first mortgage holder is foreclosing, allowing you to negotiate a short sale on the second mortgage.
- Your networking contacts tell you a specific lender has too many "nonperforming assets" on the books (i.e., too many bad loans), and you find a foreclosure property with a lien owed to this lender.
- There's a mortgage from a private party (e.g., a seller-financed note) who would be willing to take a significant discount in the amount owed just to end the emotional nightmare of the foreclosure.
- The seller has some other type of lien or private debt that's in danger of either being wiped out by the impending foreclosure or going unpaid because of the seller's financial distress.

Next, let's look at the specific steps to close a short sale.

SIX STEPS TO CLOSE A SHORT SALE

Described below are the six steps involved in closing a short sale.

Step One: Lock Up the Property Under Contract

Your first step in any short sale (indeed, your first step in any real estate deal) is to identify and meet with a motivated seller to lock up the property under contract before you spend time working with a lender to accept a short sale. If you need the short sale to make the deal profitable for you, make sure you insert a clause in your purchase contract with the seller specifically stating your agreement is contingent on the lender's accepting a short sale. That way, you can build enough profit into the deal to make it worth your time.

Here's what the legalese version of this clause reads like:

> *This agreement is "subject to" Buyer's negotiating a short sale with the existing lien holders that will allow Buyer to pay no more than $_____* [the purchase price you are willing to pay, which is less than the total owed] *total for the property. Seller acknowledges that he or she shall get NONE of the proceeds from the sale of this property other than the original deposit of $1.* [This final sentence is important because lenders will not accept a short sale if the borrower is making any profit from the sale.]

Step Two: Get Written Permission to Discuss the Loan with the Lender

Lenders won't talk with third parties unless the borrower (property owner) has signed a document expressly authorizing the lender to discuss the matter. The Authorization to Release

FIGURE 3.4 *Sample Authorization to Release Information Form*

AUTHORIZATION TO RELEASE INFORMATION

Authorization dated: _____

Borrower: _____

Property: _____

Regarding loan number: _____

To: _____
         (Lender's Name)
_____
         (Lender's Address)
_____
         (Lender's City, State, Zip)
_____
         (Lender's Phone Number)

I (We) hereby authorize you to release information regarding the above referenced loans to _____ (Authorized Party) and/or agents/assigns. This authorization or a copy of it may be sent via facsimile transmission and be fully valid and binding. This authorization is a continuing authorization for said persons or company to receive information about my (our) loan, including duplicates of any notices sent to me (us) regarding my (our) loan. In addition, I (we) hereby authorize you to discuss any aspect of our loan with Authorized Party.

Borrower	Date of Birth	Social Security Number

Information (see Figure 3.4) should be faxed to the lender as soon as possible. Typically, it takes a few days to get the authorization to discuss the loan into the lender's computer system.

Step Three: Call Lender to Open Negotiations

Before you call the seller's lender, make sure you know which department to ask for. Depending on the lender, it could be called one of the following:

- Loss mitigation department
- Loan loss mitigation department

- Loan workout department
- Foreclosure department
- Collections
- Special loans department
- Loan resolution department
- Default management department

Regardless of the name, the goal of this department is to maximize the net amount that the lender recovers from a nonperforming loan without going through the foreclosure process.

To find out whom to ask for, simply call ahead and use this script: *Hello, I'm calling to help out friends who are behind in their mortgage payments and worried about losing their house to foreclosure. Can you please tell me what department handles restructuring payments or short sales?*

Knowing the correct name of the department gives you credibility, enabling you to reach someone quickly who has the expertise and authority to help you.

Here's a sample script of your first call to the lender:

> *Investor:* Is this the _____ department? (Use the name you obtained in your initial call.)
>
> *Lender:* Yes, it is.
>
> *Investor:* Great, then this is the department that handles restructuring loan payments or short sales?
>
> *Lender:* Yes, we do. May I help you?
>
> *Investor:* I hope so. My name is Peter. Who am I talking with?
>
> *Lender:* Liz. I'm the department administrator.
>
> *Investor:* I'm very glad to meet you, Liz. I was hoping you could help me with a small matter. I just faxed over an Authorization to Release Information regarding loan number _____ and have a few quick questions for you. Do you have the authorization in your system yet?

Lender: Yes, I just pulled it up.

Investor: What needs to happen for your company to accept a short sale on a defaulted loan?

Listen carefully as the lender tells you the specific criteria you'll need to meet before this lender will accept a short sale. Each lender requires a slightly different process before accepting a short sale. Some require the borrower to go to a credit counselor first before they'll even discuss a short sale. Others require you send them a written proposal and signed contract with a seller before they'll discuss a short sale. Still others will let you negotiate the short sale right over the telephone, provided you have faxed your Authorization to Release Information. Be sure to play by the lender's rules. In fact, many lenders will fax or mail you a written outline of their specific guidelines for a short sale if you ask them.

Six tips when negotiating and working with lenders on a short sale. While every lender follows different procedures, the following powerful tips will help you successfully negotiate a short sale:

1. Keep a detailed log of all the calls and letters listing the date, time, whom you spoke with, what you discussed, and any important details you'll need later. You will always be in a stronger negotiating position if you can reference the exact history of your conversations with a lender.
2. Make sure you're dealing with the *real* lender and not a "loan-servicing" company.
3. Be sure you're negotiating with the person who has the authority to say yes. Ask if that person is able to accept the short sale or if someone else will have to make that decision.
4. Respond to *all* the lender's calls and letters. Lenders in this department are used to working with borrowers who hide and ignore their correspondence. You can build a really

strong relationship from which to negotiate a winning deal by consistently communicating with the lenders.

5. Gently remind lenders of their *real* costs to foreclose on properties. The best way is by asking questions to draw out what hassles and expenses they face if they have to foreclose, take the property back, and resell it. (See the sample script later in this chapter.)

6. As a last resort, hint at or openly discuss the "big B"—bankruptcy. When the lender learns that the borrower might be forced to declare bankruptcy if you can't work out a short sale, the lender just might have a change of heart.

Step Four: Send In Your Short-Sale Packet

If you need to send something in writing to the lender as part of your negotiation of the short sale, take the time to turn the packet into a tool to help you get a great deal. Here are the four pieces of your successful short-sale packet:

1. *Cover letter.* This letter gives the overview of what's included in the packet and why you are sending it. Highlight the condition of the house (if it's in bad shape), the seller's treatment of the house (if it looks as though the seller has stopped caring for the house), and the market for this type of property (if the market is slow in your area for this type of home). Also emphasize how your offer will provide a quick solution, allowing the lender to get cashed out in 30 days (or faster if possible). Finally, emphasize the *real* costs to the lender of having to go through the cumbersome and expensive foreclosure process.

2. *Purchase agreement.* This is the contract that says the seller agrees to sell you the property "subject to" the lender is accepting a short sale on the amount owed. Be sure this

agreement specifically states the seller will receive no money from the sale. *Lenders will not accept a short sale if the seller is making any money.*

3. *Low comparables.* Include some printed statements of what other comparable homes are selling for. Obviously, you'll select the low comparables, not the high ones. If there aren't any low comparables, skip this item.

4. *List of repairs needed and contractor-grade bids.* This list of repairs should be as extensive as possible and include bids from professional contractors for the repairs. Because most lenders will have to pay full price for professional contractors, you are letting the lenders know exactly what their expenses will be if they take the property back. Total this list and bring the message home to the lender that the property is in rough shape.

5. *Ugly photos.* Take the ugliest photos of the property you can get and include enlarged copies of these photos. This helps the lender "get" the facts of your list of repairs in an emotional way. If the house is in great shape, which is rare with foreclosures but does happen, skip the photos and list of repairs.

6. *Credibility factors (use only if they will help build your case).* If you've done short sales before, include reference letters from lenders and past homeowners. If you have good credit or lots of cash, send proof of this to support your ability to perform on your offer should the lender accept. Examples include preapproval letters from other lenders for the short-sale amount, financial statements, and credit reports.

7. *Hardship letter from the seller.* This letter should be either in the seller's own handwriting or on the seller's stationery. The seller must explain why he or she can't afford the loan anymore and describe their tough circumstances. You may have to help coach your seller to write an effective letter.

8. *Net sheet (HUD-1).* This is the draft of the settlement statement that shows the lender the exact money to be received from the closing if your short-sale proposal is accepted.

9. *Financial information on seller.* The lender often wants to see the real financial condition of the seller. This means you'll need to include copies of the seller's prior two years' tax returns, W-2s, a financial statement, etc. The lender wants to make sure the seller clearly can't afford to pay the loan.

10. *Your offer to lender.* Finally, include your formal short-sale offer to the lender. Be sure to state your offer is available for a limited time and explain why you feel you can only offer this amount of money and still conservatively make a profit.

Three criteria of irresistible short-sale offers. To make your short-sale offer irresistible to the lender, remember to emphasize the following three benefits:

1. *Fast and sure closing.* The lender's most important criterion. No 60-day or 90-day escrows; they want to finish the deal in 30 days or less.

    To help understand the short-sale process better, you can download a sample short-sale packet prepared by one of our Mentorship coaches for an actual deal. (To take advantage of this special gift from The Mentor Team, see Appendix A for details or go to *www.ForeclosureBonusPack.com* for your Bonus Web Pack.)

■ **Success Team—Commercial Coach Stephen's Story**
Not long after getting starting with the system, my wife and I negotiated our first short sale. Our mortgage agent with whom

we had done many traditional transactions referred us to a real estate agent who in the past had bad experiences with loser "investors." We were out to prove that we were not like that and were successful investors! After four phone calls, we finally talked to someone in the loss mitigation department. The house had a loan on it for approximately $139,000. The lender agreed to a short sale in the amount of $89,000. There was one catch: the lender needed that money within 15 business days—which we managed to come up with! We got an interest-only loan with no prepayment penalty for six months at about 5.8 percent. We put 5 percent of the $89,000 down—very little out of our pocket. Our exit strategy was to rehab and sell to a retail customer. The rehab money came to us from a Mentor Family member, Soft Money. We gave them 10 percent interest, and they were happy. It sold to the first retail customer who looked at the home for $175,000. After all costs, we netted $48,576. The bottom line is being ready to close fast; the lender just wants to get the deal over with. ■

2. *Cash only*! Lenders won't finance a short sale for you.
3. *No contingencies*. Lenders will be leery of short-sale offers that have so many weasel clauses; they look like Swiss cheese. One easy way around this is to use a *liquidated damages* clause to give you a pain-free, covert way to walk from the deal if worst comes to worst. (In *Making Big Money Investing in Real Estate*, we discuss liquidated damages clauses on pages 95–96 and 147–49.)

Step Five: Follow Up with Lender on the Phone

Once you have delivered your short-sale packet to the lender, don't sit back and wait for the lender to call you. Take the initiative to follow up, politely but doggedly, on your offer. Use each call as a chance to build rapport with the people in the lender's office and prod the deal one step closer to completion. Once the lender accepts your offer, move to step six.

If your offer gets turned down, this is a great chance to negotiate a deal. But before you rush in with a higher offer, pose the following question, "I understand that our offer just wasn't a fit for you. You've all been so nice about the whole thing that even if I can't get my partner to offer more, I want you to know how much I appreciate your help and professionalism. Just so I can talk with my partner about this, what's the minimum our offer would have to be for your company to even consider it?"

> **INSIDER SECRET:** Never raise the amount of money you've offered until the other side has given you a counteroffer. This allows you to take whatever the lender says as a counteroffer and use that as an entry point to negotiate a lower price. While you might not be able to get the lender to give you a definite number the decision makers would accept, usually you can get them to give you a ballpark figure that you'd have to be close to for the lender to "even consider" your offer. This is just as good as the lender giving you a definite number for your negotiating purposes.

Step Six: Close on the House

Whether you are going to close on the house yourself or flip the deal to another investor, the final step is for you to cash out the lender and buy the house. Make sure if you plan to flip the deal to someone else that you have a backup plan in place if this investor doesn't come through. Make sure you honor your word with the seller and the lender. One easy way to do this is to use a hard moneylender as a backup. You'll learn more about this, including how to interview hard moneylenders, later in Chapter 3.

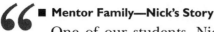

■ Mentor Family—Nick's Story

One of our students, Nick, in Salt Lake City sent us an email. Nick had been working for a pharmaceutical company until two months prior, when he quit to go into real estate investing full-time. At the time, Nick had done five deals and still owned three of the houses. He found a motivated seller who was two months behind on the payments on a beautiful two-story house. Originally, Nick structured the deal so he would net $20,000. But after attending the online training on short sales (see your Bonus Web Pack in Appendix A at end of this book), he discovered how to get a lender to say yes to a short sale. Nick talked with the lenders again and found out that the first and second mortgages were with the same company. After using the ideas from the training, Nick got the lender to accept a short sale. All totaled, Nick netted more than $110,000.   ■

Use this powerful strategy when the seller has little or no equity or even when you want to increase your profits in an ordinary foreclosure deal. You can build in your profit by solving the lender's need while solving the seller's problem, too.

LEVERAGING THE POWER OF "SUBJECT TO" WITH DISCOUNTING DEBT

One reason mastering the subject-to-existing-financing strategy is critical is that you can combine it with other buying strategies, such as discounting debt.

For example, imagine you met with a seller who's three months behind on her two mortgages. The seller owns a three-bedroom house in a working-class neighborhood. The house needs some minor cosmetic work—new carpet and paint—for it to be worth $280,000. The financial details are as follows:

Loan information:

1st mortgage of $210,000 at 6.75% interest with PITI
payments of $1,500/month

2nd mortgage of $45,000 at 12.9% interest with PI
payments of $650/month

Cost to reinstate mortgages:

1st mortgage:	$5,000
2nd mortgage:	$2,200

Market conditions:

After-repair value of house	$280,000
Cost of minor cosmetic repairs	$4,000
Market rental value	$1,700/month

If you were to analyze whether it would make sense for you to bring both loans current and purchase this house "subject to" the existing first and second mortgages, you'd probably decide that the high-interest-rate second mortgage creates a negative cash flow situation. It just wouldn't be worth doing if you left both loans in place.

Here's the three-part sequence we would coach you in to structure this deal:

1. Connect with the seller and find out why she's having problems making the payments. After talking with her using the Instant Offer System (see Chapter 5), you would discover that she has a gambling problem and is having major financial problems in other areas of her life. When you ask her what she would really like to see happen, she answers that she just wants to walk away from the house with a few thousand dollars and start fresh somewhere else. You negotiate for a while, determining that if she sold it herself and factored in closing costs, real estate commission, back payments, and

cosmetic fix-up work, she would probably owe money at the closing. At this point, the seller sighs and says that she just wants to walk away from the whole thing and be done with this nightmare.

2. Sign up the deal. You agree to make up the back payments, buy the house, and take over the property "subject to" the first and second mortgages. You create one very important contingency in the deal, though: you make sure the seller understands and agrees that the only way you're willing to move forward is if you can negotiate with the second mortgage holder to take a discounted cash payoff for the amount of money owed. Earlier, you learned that this strategy is called a *short sale*. Notice that you're looking to sell short only the second mortgage and not the low-interest-rate first mortgage, which you want to keep in place.

3. Get on the phone and call the second mortgage holder. After getting the facts on the table (i.e., the seller has a gambling problem and won't be able to pay the first or the second mortgage; the seller may have to declare bankruptcy; the house needs some fix-up work before it will even sell; etc.), you put an offer on the table for the second mortgage holder. Here's how that negotiation could go:

Investor: Of course, you could always just move forward and foreclose on the owner. Some lenders don't care about the fact that they wouldn't get much of anything after they factored in the costs to foreclose and have some investor pick up the property at a low cash price. The good thing is that we don't think this owner is the type of person who would get angry with the world and rip apart the house before the sale, just to spite you. I mean, you never know, but my gut says she's a pretty straight person. Anyway, in order to make this deal work for us, about the most we could give you for your note would be $5,000, maybe a little bit more.

Second mortgage holder: There's no way I could get my bank to accept such a low offer. You would have to do much better than that.

Investor: Boy, I can sure understand that. If I were you, I might just say, "To heck with getting any money at all, let's just foreclose to teach the owner a lesson." So I can understand that, from your view, you would need to get more money. I'm just trying to see if we can find a fit where I would even want to choose this deal over some of the other houses I'm looking at. And who knows, maybe we'll find that we just can't find a fit here. If that turns out to be the case, I want you to know that I'll be OK with that and that I really appreciate your time and openness to try to find a win-win fit here. What would be the lowest amount you could take to make this acceptable to your bank, knowing that it still needs to be low enough to work for us as investors?

Second mortgage holder: I don't see how we could accept less than $10,000 for the note.

Investor: Really [*scrunching up your face to get the right tonality of incredulity and disappointment*], the lowest you could take is $8,000 to 10,000? [Notice you just used the range technique here.]

Second mortgage holder: Well, we might take as little as $9,000 . . . but we'd need to have it in certified funds within 21 days.

Together we just negotiated a $36,000 discount off the second mortgage! This is pure profit for you in the deal. But wait, you say, you don't have that much cash to put in the deal. After you add up the $4,000 of cosmetic fix-up, the $5,000 to bring the first mortgage current, $2,000 in closing costs, and the $9,000 to pay off the second mortgage, that totals $20,000. You just don't have that kind of money. That's a challenge, but it's not insurmountable. Just as we don't put money into the first two deals we take all the way to the bank on a joint-venture basis with our Mentorship students, we're not going to send you a check for the $20,000, either! But soon we'll share several powerful techniques to cultivate sources of funding for your deals.

Let's get clear on your motivation to find the $20,000 to fund this deal. You will be getting a house on which you'll have permanent, long-term financing in place at 6.75 percent interest. After you subtract all the costs, you'll have an instant equity position based on the $280,000 value of $47,000, *and* the house will generate a positive cash flow of at least $200 a month. Have we tapped into your greed glands deeply enough to spark you into finding a way to fund this deal?

Following are six ways to fund this deal (some you've already read about, some you will come across later in this book):

1. Sell the house with owner financing, collecting a 10 percent down payment. This will get you $28,000 cash up front plus a great monthly cash flow and a large back-end profit.
2. Get a cash advance on one or more credit cards to fund the deal and then sell the house outright to a retail buyer.
3. Use your own money to fund this deal, knowing the profit will ensure a very high return on investment.
4. Borrow the money from a private lender and pay a fair rate of return on that money with the interest to accrue so you can protect your cash flow.
5. Partner with another investor who will put up the money and split the profits with you.
6. Wholesale the deal to another investor for $10,000 cash.

Are you getting into the spirit here? The key to remember is that if the deal is good enough, you will find the money. You were able to take a deal that many investors wouldn't have the skill to make work and turn it into a huge moneymaker for yourself by combining "subject-to" financing with discounting the debt owed.

Many investors look only for properties with lots of equity. You've already learned how to make a healthy profit by using the short-sale technique. Here is another way to use that technique to make even more money. The next time you review the title report on a property you're buying and find any liens against the property you weren't aware of, don't panic. You just might have a great opportunity to make more money by buying those other liens for pennies on the dollar.

■ Success Team—Coach Robb's Story

We were helping a Mentorship student structure a deal on a $250,000 house that was in preforeclosure. The seller owed roughly $180,000 and wanted to get enough money from the sale to pay off $40,000 in debt that he had. Most of the debt was medical bills from a health situation several months back. We recommended that the student sign up the deal, agreeing that she would make up the $8,000 of back payments and buy the property "subject to" the first mortgage of $180,000. The student would also agree to satisfy all the other outstanding hospital bills the seller had accumulated.

We then recommended the student get written permission from the seller to negotiate the outstanding bill with the hospital. We felt that the student could get that $40,000 of debt settled for as little as $10,000 to $15,000 *and* could work out a payment plan with the bank to pay that money over the course of 12 to 36 months. ■

In this case, dealing with the seller's bills meant an extra $25,000 to $30,000 of profit, made in a way that allowed the seller to win, too. What other types of liens against the property can you discount? Remember, don't just think about debt as money owed to a lender on a mortgage. You can negotiate discounts on just about any lien against the property, or as you saw in the previous example, you can also negotiate bills the seller has that aren't even technically liens against the property and *still* get the seller to give you full credit for that money as if you'd paid the seller the face value of the debt.

You can discount things such as the following:

- Mechanics' liens for work done on a house
- Personal judgments against a homeowner
- Personal debts (e.g., medical bills, credit card debt)
- Business debts

Following are two key considerations to help determine if the lien holder will accept less than what's owed:

1. *How unsure of collection is the creditor?* How likely (or unlikely) is the creditor actually to get any money from the debtor? Is a lot of equity protecting the lien? Or is the lien likely to get completely wiped out in a foreclosure sale? Maybe the debt isn't even secured against the property, in which case the creditor will probably be even more willing to discount deeper. Is it a first mortgage (in the most secure position and therefore the hardest to discount) or is it in third position after two other mortgages? You get the idea here. The more the debt is at risk, the deeper the discount you should go after.

2. *How badly does the creditor need the money?* Obviously, a roofer whose cash-flow situation is tight will be more likely to give you a discount than a large mortgage lender. So find out as much as you can about the people who are owed the money.

INSIDER SECRET: Many states have laws prohibiting unlicensed contractors from filing any type of lien against properties. Depending on the law in your state, if an unlicensed contractor did not get paid, he or she may not legally be able to record a mechanic's lien against the property's title. If the contractor did file a lien, it would not be enforceable in court. This is another example of why it's important to know the laws in your state. (We encourage you to begin your research with the summary of your state's laws included in your Bonus Web Pack located in Appendix A of this book.)

■ Success Team—Coach Juli's Story

I always ask the sellers not only what they owe against the property, but *who* they owe it to. I have found that private parties are much more willing to take significantly less than what they're owed just to get their money fast. That's why I love buying properties where the prior seller carried back a large first or second mortgage; many times, they're willing to discount this note if the current seller is behind in payments. Never underestimate the power of "cash now." I don't even think it's about greed on the prior seller's part; it's much more about relief. They just want to be able to get a clean break from that house they thought they had sold years ago.   ■

Imagine you found a seller who had a $360,000 house and was $10,000 behind on the first mortgage of $320,000. Also, there were two liens against the property: a mechanic's lien for $18,000 for the new roof and $15,000 owed to an ex-husband as part of a divorce settlement.

First, you call the roofer to see what you can do:

> *Ring, ring . . .*
> *Roofer:* Hello.
> *Investor:* Hi, this is Ian, is Ralph there?
> *Roofer:* This is Ralph. What can I do for you?
> *Investor:* Oh great. It sounds like I caught you in the middle of something?

Roofer: No, I was just organizing things for my next job. What can I do for you?

Investor: Actually, I was calling because I'm an investor who sometimes buys notes and liens that look like they'll be wiped out in a pending foreclosure or bankruptcy. I'm sure you probably knew about how the Sutton Street house you have a mechanic's lien on is about to be foreclosed on any day now. It looks like you aren't the only one the owner didn't pay. I don't know if there's any reason for us to be talking or not about my buying your lien for a cash payment. You probably wouldn't even want to talk to me about my handing you a cashier's check in the next 14 to 30 days for your outstanding bill on that property, huh?

Roofer: You mean you'd pay me cash for that lien? Why would you want to do that?

Investor: Well, it wouldn't be because I'm just a nice person. I mean, I am a nice person, but I want to be clear here that's not why I would get you cash, if I decided it would even work for me. Like I said, I'm an investor who buys liens and notes that look like they are about to be foreclosed out and then I aggressively go after making money from the note. The way I figure it, I know that if I get a big enough discount in exchange for getting someone like yourself a cash payment, then the big gamble I'm taking pays off for me on enough of these things that I make a nice living doing this. But boy, you probably wouldn't even want to talk about selling your note for a discount, huh?

Roofer: Yes, I would. How much would you give me for the note?

Investor: To be frank, I'm not even sure if I want to buy this note or not. May I ask you a few questions to see if this is even a note that I would want to buy?

Roofer: Sure, I'd be glad to answer any questions. [*Notice how the conversation has turned and you, the investor, are in the driver's seat where you belong. Now it's time to build the lien holder's motivation to sell.*]

Investor: What have you done to collect on this note in the past?

Roofer: We tried invoicing the owner for about two months. And I went over to the property to collect the money three times myself.

Investor: And that worked [*big eyes*]?

Roofer: No, he wouldn't even open the door and talk with me.

Investor: Really? Tell me about what that was like? [*Voice getting softer and using scrunchy face*]

Roofer: I was so pissed off at the guy. I mean, I took three guys off another job to fit in the roof on his house, and then he stiffs me. I started banging on the door, and he shouts out that he's called the cops on me. I just took off.

Investor: What did you do then to collect?

Roofer: I filed the paperwork for the mechanic's lien, and I figure he'll have to pay me someday.

Investor: How does that mechanic's lien thing work? Does it mean he has to pay you off in 30 days or something [*big eyes*]?

Roofer: No, basically it means it's a lien against the property; so before he sells it, he'll have to get me to sign off on some papers, or he can't sell it. So he'll have to pay me plus interest before I'll sign.

Investor: That makes sense . . . And so if the bank moves ahead with the foreclosure, he'll just pay you at the foreclosure sale?

Roofer: No, if it goes to foreclosure, I probably won't get paid at all. I'd have to take him to court and get a judgment for what he owes me and then try to collect on that.

Investor: Oh, OK. Well, I'm not sure if this is a lien I'm going to want. It sounds like the chances of collecting are less than I originally anticipated. If I were willing to buy the lien from you for cash, what would you do with the money?

Roofer: The money would be going back into my business, which had to cover our costs for the roof. I had to pay for the guys and most of the materials. I still kick myself for not getting a larger deposit up front from the guy.

Investor: Well, at least you're lucky enough to have your business going so well that you don't really need the money. It just may be your better option to sit tight and hope he makes good on the 10 grand he owes the bank in late payments, and then in a year or two, he may refinance the property and pay you off or something, right?

Roofer: Doubtful. He's the kind of jerk who would end up losing the house to the bank. How much are you willing to pay me for the lien?

Investor: Oh, well, I'm not sure if I would want to buy it or not yet. I mean if you wanted some huge amount of money like $7,000 or $10,000 for the lien, then obviously that wouldn't work for me. What's the least you would take for the lien, knowing that this would have to work for you, but it would also have to work for me as an investor taking a mighty big risk here? $700? $1,000? Or maybe a little bit more?

Roofer: I'd never sell it for that little; it just wouldn't be worth it. I'd need to get at least $5,000 for it.

Investor: Really [*scrunchy face*]. $3,000 to $5,000 is the least you'd take? [*Range technique*] Are you sure you couldn't go lower?

Roofer: No, I wouldn't take any less.

And away you go. You just got the note for $3,000 and were able to pocket the other $15,000 as extra equity that goes along with your purchase of the house. The call probably took you 20 minutes, tops. Where else can you make $15,000 in 20 minutes on the phone?

But wait, you're not done yet. You still have that $15,000 owed to the ex-husband! If you follow the previous ideas, you'll probably be able to buy that note for even less. Why? Because the ex-spouse likely never expects to get paid that money anyway. The ex-spouse probably lives out of state and will be thrilled to get any money you pay now and get closure to the situation. You might even get the note for as little as $500 to $1,500, which would make you another $13,500 to $14,500 on the house the moment you buy it.

Now do you understand why notes and liens and judgments can often be a great profit source for you in a foreclosure deal? Savvy investors know that the more little liens and private debt a seller owes, the more profit that may mean for the investor.

You negotiate with the seller as if these debts couldn't be discounted and were at face value, but you know you can get them for pennies on the dollar later by negotiating directly with the creditor.

■ Success Team—Commercial Coach Rob's Story

I recently got an email from Paul, one of our students. Paul owns a cleaning business, and one of his employees was losing her $60,000 home to foreclosure. She had a first mortgage for $13,000 and a second mortgage for $25,000 and owed $2,000 to a local hospital. All together, Paul was looking at buying the house for $40,000.

He talked with the second mortgage holder and offered the decision makers $7,000 for the note. They countered him at $9,000. Paul went back and asked them to meet him in the middle at $8,000. They agreed. Next, he called up the hospital administrators and offered them $500 for their bill. After having their board review the offer, they accepted. All totaled, Paul went on to have a positive cash flow by renting the house for three years before selling it for a $30,000 net profit. Over the past four years, Paul has built up a net worth of a million dollars and a monthly cash flow of $10,000 from his investment activities.   ■

WHY EVERY INVESTOR—INCLUDING YOU— CAN BE A CASH BUYER

Many investors mistakenly believe t͡ with cash is by having perfect credit for borrowing having the liquid cash sitting in a bank to tap into. We hope you ͘ already seen that this just isn't true. You've learned about "subject to" financing, flipping deals, and discounting liens. You've learned that sometimes you can get the seller some or all of his or her equity out in cash and buy "subject to" the seller's loan. And you've learned about flipping deals that get the seller cash—and get you cash, too! Now it's time to learn the seven sources for funding your deals, listed in the order that most investors prefer them.

SEVEN SOURCES OF FUNDING FOR DEALS OTHER THAN YOUR LOCAL BANK

The following seven funding sources are listed in the order of desirability for you, the investor.

Source One: The Seller

The single best source to fund the deal is the seller. We know this might sound strange. After all, isn't the seller so financially strapped that he or she can't even make the monthly payment? Well, yes, but remember the seller has existing financing in place and, in some cases, has equity in the house to lend you.

You've heard of using other people's money (OPM). Now understand the true power of other people's mortgages (OPMs). That's what "subject to" financing really is—using other people's mortgages to make you wealthy.

This isn't complicated; "subject to" financing is the seller's being your bank, at least functionally. And the seller is even more obviously your source of funding when he or she agrees to take a note for part or all of the money you have agreed to from your purchase of the property.

Source Two: Your Buyer

Depending on how you plan to sell the property, you can generate immediate cash to fund your deal from a few thousand dollars to hundreds of thousands of dollars. You'll find many more details on how to make this part of the deal work in Chapter 7 and Chapter 8, but for the moment, it's important to understand that your buyer can be a great source of funding for your deals.

If you sell the property on a rent-to-own basis, you can typically collect 1 percent to 5 percent of the purchase price as a nonrefundable option payment. If you are selling with owner financing (e.g., land contract, wraparound mortgage, all-inclusive trust deed [AITD]—all explained in Chapter 8), you can typically collect 10 percent to 15 percent down. And if you structure the deal in which your buyer brings in a new first mortgage, then you can generally get *all* the money you need to fund a cash purchase of the property owned by your motivated seller who was in foreclosure.

Let's look closely at this final way to use your buyer's money to fund your way into the deal. Let's start with an example.

Imagine you meet a motivated seller who is in foreclosure and about four weeks from losing her house at auction. She owns a four-bedroom, two-and-a-half-bath house in a nice part of town. The seller admits she has been living in denial for the past five months and now finally realizes something has to happen fast.

The house, worth $300,000, is in great shape; all you have to do to get it in showing condition is to have it professionally cleaned. It has an existing first mortgage of $180,000. You meet with the seller and, using the simple five-step system in Chapter 5, negotiate an all-cash price of $220,000, with you paying all closing costs. You feel great about negotiating a price that's $80,000 below market value, but you're scared about where you'll get the $220,000.

Here's one way to make this deal happen. You resell the property *before* you close on it with the seller. That is, you put it on the market for $280,000 and offer to help your buyer finance the purchase. Have your buyer get a 90-5-5 loan, which means that person brings in a new loan for 90 percent of the purchase price ($252,000) and puts 5 percent down ($14,000). You carry back a 5 percent second mortgage ($14,000).

It's a win-win-win solution. Your buyer, who probably has less-than-perfect credit, wins by both saving $20,000 on the price and having your help on the financing. Your seller both saves her credit and salvages $40,000 of equity. Best of all, she will never have to look back again. And here's what you'd make on this deal:

Purchase price	$220,000
Selling price	$280,000
Gross profit	**$60,000**

Look at what you net and when you get that money:

Gross profit	$60,000
Closing costs	($3,000)
Cleanup	($500)
Advertising	($500)
Net profit	**$56,000**

All totaled, you net $56,000 on the deal. You get $42,000 cash at the closing in the form of a check you get from the title or escrow company. And you have a second mortgage for the other $14,000.

In this example, your buyer is making you 12 percent interest-only payments on that note with a balloon note due for the

$14,000 in three years. That means each month you collect a check for $140, and in three years your buyer will give you a lump-sum payment of $14,000—cash your buyer will most likely get by refinancing the house.

You'll learn more about how to sell houses like this quickly in Chapter 7, but for now, understand that you *can* handle this deal—an all-cash deal—without any cash or credit of your own. In real estate, you get paid for the specialized knowledge you bring to a deal. That knowledge lets you do things most sellers don't have the expertise to do and most real estate agents don't have the experience or comfort level to do.

Isn't it reasonable that once you get good at this game, you'll be able to find someone who wants to buy a nice house for $20,000 below value, especially when you are willing to participate in the financing to make the deal work?

You can also use your buyer's money to fund your way into a deal in which you need to get the seller a small down payment. Because you can sell the house with owner financing and typically collect 10 percent down, you can often get the seller a chunk of money for his or her equity and buy the property "subject to" the existing financing. The seller gets all the cash he or she expected from the deal up front; the buyer gets a house without bank-qualifying hassles; you make a healthy profit for being the matchmaker between the two parties.

■ Success Team—Peter's Story

I was talking with Marcia, one of our Mentorship alumni students from five years ago. Marcia told me about a deal she made with a motivated seller who called her after seeing a small classified ad she ran. The seller was $1,500 behind on his $35,000 mortgage. Marcia bought his house "subject to" the existing financing and used the $5,000 option payment she collected from her tenant-buyer to pay for the back payments and for the other $1,500 the deal cost her. Marcia still owns that house, which generates a $200 positive cash flow each month. It's an example of funding the deal with her buyer's money.   ■

Source Three: Your Money or Lines of Credit

If the amount of money you need is small enough that you can comfortably fund the deal, and if the deal is good enough to warrant putting your own money into the deal, then seize the opportunity.

Here are two considerations to take into account before funding deals yourself:

1. Is the amount of money you're putting into the deal small enough that you feel comfortable taking the risk of losing it? If the answer is no, look for a different source of funding.

2. Are you experienced enough investing that you feel comfortable putting more of your money or credit on the line to fund the deal? If you've paid your dues, invested in your real estate education, and completed some deals, then you're qualified to put your own money or credit on the line. Remember, sometimes having money or access to money through your lines of credit is a detriment to your creation of wealth. Easy access to money can often make early deals too easy to obtain. If they were harder to fund, you might decide to pass on marginal deals altogether. You cannot make up for a lack of knowledge and experience with money and *not* expect to pay a healthy price for learning that lesson.

■ **Success Team—Coach Emily's Story**

While reading through postings on our Mentorship student website, I came across one from Byron, a member of The Mentor Family. In his posting, he gave his formula for how much to discount the money you pay to a seller when you have to make up back payments on a house you're buying "subject to" the existing financing. His formula was to lower the money paid for the house by $3 to $4 for each $1 you have to put into the deal up front to catch up the back payments. Therefore, if you put $5,000 into the deal to catch up the back payments, Byron recommends you get at least a $15,000 to $20,000 discount off the purchase price of the house. I looked back over the deals I had bought "subject to" and recognized that I followed his formula most of the time. And the times I didn't, I regretted it.   ■

With that cautionary point made, we think that many times it does make sense for you to fund your own deals, especially when you're talking about making up some back payments and taking over "subject to" the existing financing. Following are three sources of cash open to many investors:

1. *Credit cards.* Cash advances are a fast source of cash.
2. *Home equity loans.* Smart investors set up these lines of tax-deductible credit before they need them.
3. *Pension plans.* Many 401(k) plans allow you to borrow money from the plan and repay it later, paying interest into your tax-deferred plan. Self-directed IRAs are also great vehicles for investing in real estate, especially Roth IRAs.

Source Four: Private Lenders

By private lenders, we don't mean banks or hard moneylenders. Rather, we recommend starting to cultivate relationships with people who can fund deals for you in exchange for your paying them a fair interest rate on their money.

■ Success Team—Peter's Story

Finding the right private lenders becomes even more important when you move up to investing in Level Three deals like commercial properties. Recently, some of our Commercial Mentorship students found a deal worth working on. It was a piece of land with a building designated for a specific use. The property was worth $15 million, but using our negotiating strategies, they were able to put the property under contract for $7.6 million. There was a catch—they had to raise $5 million in 30 days. They actually raised the necessary funding from private investors. Now they have subdivided the property and are working on getting it rezoned. They are selling it off piece by piece for more than twice the $7.6 million that they paid for it.

If you asked them if it was worthwhile to develop relationships with private lenders to fund deals, what do you think they would tell you?   ■

Following is a list of people you can approach about funding deals for you:

- Family
- Friends
- People on fixed incomes who need greater returns than CDs and money market accounts can give them
- Other investors who deal in real estate and are willing to get a fair return on a first or second mortgage. (Note: The people you want for good rates will almost always want a first mortgage with good equity protecting them.)

Imagine you are talking with a family friend about your investing. You know this person has retired and is living fairly comfortably on his or her investments. He or she could be a potential private lender for your real estate business. Here's a script of what to say to a potential private lender:

Potential private lender: So you have been investing in foreclosures for how long now?

Investor: Well, it's been about seven months now since I got started. Funny enough, it all started from a book I picked up while browsing in the bookstore.

Potential private lender: How's it been going so far?

Investor: I'm really pleased with the way things have been going. I've done four deals so far. The first deal I found was a foreclosure that I flipped to another investor. The deal was good, but I was a bit scared to fully commit to the deal. I got $12,000 for assigning this other investor my contract to purchase the property. He closed on the house and rehabbed it and resold it two months later and made $43,000. The next two houses I still have. And the last deal I picked up three weeks ago. I'm in the final stages of fixing it up and then will sell it to a retail buyer. I expect to make around $30,000 on that one.

Potential private lender: Wow! That's great. I'm really happy for you.

Investor: Yeah, in fact the more deals I do, the more I realize that the only thing slowing me down is needing to cultivate private lenders who want to fund a deal where there's plenty of security in it for them and a fair rate of return on their money. Hey, maybe you know someone who has some money in a CD or in a money market account who would like to earn a healthy rate of return secured by a first mortgage on a house with at least 25 percent to 30 percent equity protecting the loan?

Potential private lender: Actually, I might be interested in funding a deal if it really was secure enough for me. What interest rate would you give me?

Investor: May I ask you a question first? [*softer tone and voice now*] Why would you even want to fund a deal?

Potential private lender: With interest rates where they're at, I'm only getting 5.5 percent on my 12-month CDs. If you can give me a higher interest rate and it's really a safe investment, then I'd like to get a better rate of return.

Investor: That makes sense. What type of interest rate did you hope to make?

Potential private lender: I don't know—8 percent to 10 percent would be great.

Investor: OK, actually that's about what I thought would be fair to pay a private lender for using their money to fund a deal. . . .

See how easy that was? Don't try to sell private lenders on some high rate of return. Let them tell you what interest rate they think would be fair. You'll be shocked at how many will mention a number that's well below what you might have volunteered before reading this book.

Following are the top four concerns of private lenders:

1. Security
2. Security
3. Security
4. Reasonable interest rate and security (They tie for fourth place!)

We hope this drives the point home. Many investors make the mistake of approaching individuals they know about funding a deal, then trying to sell this potential private lender on a high rate of return on their money or on the ease of the transaction. Neither of these is important to private lenders. They want to make sure their investment is safe. That's why high rates of interest actually scare private lenders away. After all, they say, if the investor is willing to pay 15 percent interest, this deal must be risky.

So speak to the private lender's fear of losing money first, second, third, and fourth!

This means conveying the following three things:

1. *Assurance that you've done this before.* It's difficult to get money from private lenders (other than "love money" from family members) unless you have successfully done a few deals. The better your track record, the safer your private lender feels.

2. *An understanding of what's protecting the lenders in the deal.* Make sure you show the prospective private lenders the appraisal on the property or comparable homes that sold to substantiate the equity that will protect their loan. Let them know they'll be protected—just as a bank is with a recorded mortgage or deed of trust. Encourage them to take all the paperwork to their attorney for review to make sure it's all on the up-and-up. Show them actual photos of the house, or better yet, take them to the house and talk them through your plans while walking through it.

3. *Show private lenders your exit strategy on paper.* Include your detailed financial analysis of how you plan to make enough from the deal to pay back their money. (This document is called a *pro forma analysis*.)

You might be saying, "This sounds like a lot of work," and you'd be correct. It *is* a lot of work. The advantage is that once you help these private lenders make money once, they'll start to trust you, and your next deal will be much easier. In fact, if you treat your private investors right, and this means *never, ever* letting them lose money, they will tell their friends and associates about you. This could mean you'll never struggle to fund a deal again. It may take you 12 to 18 months to get to this point, but it's worth it.

■ **Success Team—Commercial Coach Cleve's Story**

Mike, one of my Commercial Mentoring students, found it hard to believe that he could buy large properties using private investors' money. He looked scared when I coached him to "sign it up and if it's a great deal, the money won't be a problem." However, Mike followed my advice and purchased an 80-unit apartment building in Houston, Texas, without using any of his own money.   ■

 ■ **Success Team—Coach Mike's Story**

I received an email from Paul, a student who had bought a home-study course we offer on buying homes "subject to" the existing financing. Paul bumped into a motivated seller in a 7-Eleven store. This seller had a rental property he needed to sell fast.

The house was worth $170,000, and the seller owed $73,000 on a first mortgage plus $24,000 of back payments. Paul signed up the deal "subject to" the existing financing using the forms from our course. He borrowed $40,000 from a private lender to pay the back payments on the house and fund the fix-up work it needed. (His private lender was his mother-in-law who had gotten tired of losing money in the stock market!) Paul still has the house as a rental property, which generates $800 a month of positive cash flow. He currently has $42,000 of equity in the house. One year ago, Paul took the leap and left his job with the federal government to go into real estate investing full-time. He's never looked back.   ■

Source Five: Money Partners

In addition to finding people to lend money in exchange for a guaranteed interest rate, you can find other investors who would like to partner on a deal. They provide the funding for the deal—either by putting in their own money or by borrowing the money based on their credit and income—and you put in the work. You then "split" the deal.

You can split deals in many ways. You could joint-venture on the house on a 50-50 basis. You can split money with any proceeds from the sale of the house first going to repay the cash investment of the money partner, then with 25 percent of the net profit going to your money partner and 75 percent going to you. You can structure the deal any way that wins for both of you.

Four things to be careful of when you bring in a money partner. Take special care in the following four areas when bringing in a money partner:

1. *Put all the details in writing.* A clearly written agreement is essential to creating a smooth business relationship. Your agreement should spell out the details of who is responsible for what parts of the deal, how you'll handle funding for the deal, how you'll split profits, and how to end the relationship if it doesn't work out.
2. *Be careful of a general partnership.* A general partnership, the default business relationship unless you set up another one, means each party is 100 percent responsible for all the liability, yet each party only gets a portion of the profit. Consider using a limited liability company (LLC) or a limited partnership to lower your risk.
3. *Check references.* Always know with whom you're doing business. Have these partners lived up to their word in the past? How did they react to conflict and stressful times in the past?
4. *Make sure you have control or at least a recorded interest.* If the deal is for real, your partner should always be willing to have you record a *memorandum of agreement* to protect your interest (or if you are the one in control, then you should be willing to record something to protect your partner's interest).

Source Six: Hard Moneylenders

Imagine you find a great buy on a foreclosure house. The house in our example needs $40,000 of rehab work and has an after-repair value of $400,000. You negotiated well with the owner and locked up a price of $230,000. That's more than $100,000 of potential profit, even after you factor in holding costs, closing costs, and all the rest. (Heck, it's almost enough to make us want to take on the rehab project! Almost . . . We'd still probably sell the deal to another investor for a cash assignment fee, but that's just us.)

But you wonder, "How can I get the $230,000 to buy the property, plus the money for closing costs, plus the $40,000 to rehab the property?" Consider a source of financing called a *hard moneylender*. We know this term conjures up images of a loan shark with a muscle-bound companion ready to make you pay up or else, but that's not true at all. Hard moneylenders have a large pool of cash they're willing to lend to investors who are buying real estate in situations with enough equity in the properties that they consider the loans safe.

When you are borrowing from hard moneylenders, they won't care what your credit is like, or how much money you earn, or the size of your bank account. They care about one thing only—is there enough equity in the property to secure the loan? In fact, one benefit to hard money loans (beyond the obvious part of not having loan applications to fill out or credit reports pulled) is that often you won't have to guarantee the loan personally. The property itself will be the sole source of collateral of the loan, not your good credit. Of course, you'll have to pay some hefty costs to get this money.

Following are three things you pay a hard moneylender for the loan:

1. *Higher than market interest rates.* Most hard moneylenders will charge you 12 percent to 15 percent interest on the money you borrow.

2. *Points.* Points represent a fee you are charged up front for the loan. One point is equal to 1 percent of the loan amount. Typically, you'll have to pay a hard moneylender at least five to ten points up front for the loan. The only good news about points is that you can usually roll them into your loan so you can "pay" them with borrowed money.

3. *Prepayment penalty.* Hard moneylenders know that when they charge such high interest rates on the money they lend, investors who borrow from them are highly motivated either to resell the property or refinance the property to pay off the high-interest-rate loan as quickly as possible. Hard moneylenders don't get all that available cash by being dumb; many put a prepayment penalty into the loan that says, "If you pay off the loan before a certain date, you have to pay up to six months' interest."

Let's look at what these costs mean in our current example. First, your hard moneylender will charge you five points on your $270,000 loan, which comes to $13,500. Plus you'll have $2,000 of closing costs, which your friendly neighborhood hard moneylender will let you add into the loan amount. Finally, you'll have to pay 15 percent interest on the property, which you got the hard moneylender to agree to let "accrue." This means you don't have to pay each month while you're rehabbing and reselling the property; the interest charges will simply be added to the principal balance you owe. Thankfully, you got away without having to pay a prepayment penalty.

Now you close on the house using $230,000 of the lender's money, plus a little more for closing costs, and get to work on the rehab. A hard moneylender isn't going to give you the whole $40,000 up front for the rehab work; that would put the lender in a bad position if you just took that money and didn't do any work. Instead, that money will be paid out to you (either through an escrow fund or directly from the hard moneylender) as you need it to pay for completed work or for materials needed to get a chunk of the work done.

Two months later, your rehab is complete. Congratulations! You put the house on the market. Because you want a fast sale, you list the house with a quality real estate agent in your area for $399,980. Sixty-eight days later, you close with your buyer for $392,000. After you pay all your costs, you net more than $75,000. It took a lot of work on your part to coordinate all the contractors and keep your real estate agent working fast to get the house sold, but in the end it was worth it. In fact, for years to come, every time you drive past that house, you'll get that warm fuzzy $75,000 feeling!

With all these costs, why wouldn't you just go to your local bank and get the decision makers to lend you the $270,000? Good question. The answer is that a conventional lender won't lend you money based on the after-repair value. In fact, a conventional lender won't lend you money based on the *market* value. A conventional lender will lend you money based on the current value or your purchase price—whichever is *lower*. This means even if you lock up a $100,000 price on a house that has a current "as is" value of $170,000, the lender will only lend you money based on the $100,000 purchase price. You lose the benefit of counting that $70,000 worth of equity as part of the consideration of whether the lender will lend to you or not. In addition, a conventional lender is almost always going to want to see a 10 percent to 20 percent down payment from you, the investor, even if you have substantial equity already in place.

We know this seems crazy, but that's just the way it works. We didn't make the rules, which is one of the reasons we avoid working with conventional lenders when we can. Hard money lenders will make loans based on the "as is" value or based off the after-repair value, depending on what you arrange with them. Because they'll maintain a low enough loan-to-value ratio to protect themselves in case you default, they won't require a credit check or proof of income. You can actually get a hard money loan even if you went bankrupt four months ago and have been out of work for the past seven years!

What amount of equity will hard moneylenders require to protect themselves in this loan? Generally, they'll lend up to 70 percent or 75 percent loan-to-value. This means there will need to be at least 25 percent to 30 percent equity protecting the lender's loan.

Also, when borrowing from a hard moneylender, it will take 48 to 72 hours to cut you a cashier's check. Compare that to borrowing from your local bank, which can take up to 30 to 60 days to "rush" your loan through. When you're buying foreclosure property this far below market value, fast access to cash is everything.

■ Success Team—Peter's Story

I got a call from my student Cheryl who said her real estate agent located an REO property that Cheryl had a contract on to buy for $105,000. Because the average retail value (ARV) of the house was $135,000 and the house only needed $5,000 of repairs, I got excited for her. She asked if I wanted to fund the deal as a hard moneylender. Because I had made other loans to her in the past (not to mention having bought a dozen houses with her over the years), I agreed. The point is that sometimes successful investors make a great source of hard money loans. ■

INSIDER SECRET: Finding the right hard moneylender is important for your foreclosure investing business. Here is a script to help find the right hard moneylender (but only when you need one).

You: Hi, my name is _____, and I'm calling in response to your ad for loans. I'm an investor who buys and fixes up properties. I'm calling several hard moneylenders before choosing one to fund my properties in this area. Can I ask you some questions about the loans you make?

- What type of interest rate are you offering right now?
- Do you charge points, and if so, how many?
- What are any other costs I'd incur as a part of the loan?
- How long do you structure the loans to be?
- Do you prefer interest-only payments?
- What is the loan-to-value ratio that you prefer to stay within?
- Is that based on the repaired value or the "as-is" value?
- How much does credit affect your decisions to fund a loan?
- How long does it typically take to fund a loan?
- What questions do you have for me?
- What would I need to do in order to give you an opportunity to lend on one of my properties?

Source Seven: VA and HUD Foreclosures

One niche area of foreclosures is buying Department of Veterans Affairs (VA) and Department of Housing and Urban Development (HUD) foreclosures. These government agencies help people buy homes by guaranteeing loans to the lenders. In some cases, the borrowers default on the loan payments, and the lenders foreclose. After the foreclosure process winds its way to completion, these agencies (VA and HUD) end up with the properties. They want to sell these properties as easily and quickly as possible, so many times, they give investors with good credit and income great deals on price and terms.

Many of these properties end up with these agencies because the agencies offer programs that help buyers get into homes with low down payments and fairly loose credit standards. Both of these factors help increase the default rate of borrowers with these types of loans. It also means there isn't enough equity in the properties to entice investors to buy them at the foreclosure auction.

It's an established fact that the lower the amount of equity homeowners have, the higher the rate of default on their loans. It makes sense. The lower the equity a homeowner has, the less the person has at stake in the house, and the higher the monthly payments will be (compared with a homeowner who has a lower loan balance and more equity).

Herein lies your opportunity. These agencies want to entice people to bid on their foreclosed houses. One way they do this (besides selling the house for a discount on what it is worth) is by agreeing to provide the financing needed to purchase one of these properties. Many times, they'll even let investors buy with as little as 5 percent down to cover all the closing costs. Considering that most investors need to put 20 percent to 25 percent down plus have cash to cover closing costs to secure traditional financing, this proposition can be appealing.

■ Success Team—Peter's Story

I saw a duplex that was a HUD foreclosure advertised on the weekly HUD listing in my local paper. The vacant property was in an area I knew would be good for a rental. HUD provided 5 percent down financing for investors so I decided to bid on the property. My bid of $80,000 was accepted. Over the next 10 years, I kept the property as a rental with a positive cash flow. Then I sold it for $245,000. I kick myself when I realize I could have bought five more just like that one. Learn from this mistake. Don't sit back and *think* about investing; get out there and do it.   ■

Be aware of the following four downsides to these types of deals:

1. *They require getting traditional bank loans.* You'll need to have the credit and income to qualify for the financing (not to mention the hassle of dealing with the application process).

2. *You have to purchase these properties "as is."* This means you need a clear understanding of the condition of the property. With most homes you buy, the sellers have certain disclosure obligations; these agencies don't have to live up to the same standards.

3. *You'll be limited on the number of these types of houses you can qualify for, using their financing.* For some reason (possibly the statistically higher default ratio), these agencies will cut off your ability to buy using their financing after three to five houses. If you have the financial resources to take advantage of these programs, make sure you pick only the very best deals. You'd hate to see a marginal house you bought keep you from buying a home run of a house because you couldn't find another source to fund the deal.

4. *Sometimes the ease with which you can purchase these houses encourages investors to get lazy.* And lazy investors often fail to conduct their due diligence to make sure the deal is worthwhile.

Buying VA foreclosures can be a great entry point into investing or an added tool in your investing toolbox. But sometimes the easy ways of buying aren't the smartest. With the easy financing the VA provides (at least it's easy on the first three to five houses you buy; then it typically becomes much harder to get), you buy at a price that's higher than one you'd pay all cash for.

But wait. You say you didn't pay all cash, that you used the bank's money with 5 percent down to cover closing costs (e.g., real estate agent's commission, escrow fees, etc.). This is one of the biggest mistakes investors make when buying using traditional financing. They forget that when they personally sign on a loan, they are really cash buyers. And cash buyers should get a *big* discount for paying cash.

Again, wait. How can we say you're paying cash when you only have 5 percent down and most of that covers closing costs?

Any time you're borrowing the money so the seller gets all of the cash at the closing (whether it's from your bank account or your lender's bank account), you're buying with cash. Don't think the money has to be all yours; the important point of view here is the seller's.

When the VA provides the financing, you'll have to personally sign on the loan. The VA is not going to let you sign on behalf of your corporation or limited liability company (LLC). Therefore, we believe you should consider VA purchases as all-cash sales. Remembering this will help keep you sharp and hungry when you're negotiating to get the right price up front.

■ Success Team—Peter's Story

I will be the first to admit I've made mistakes when buying VA foreclosures. In fact, I remember one property I bought with a partner and ended up paying $25,000 too much. After owning it for about a year, I sold it at breakeven to my costs. No matter what your real estate agent thinks you should offer or how easy the financing is to obtain, make sure you're really buying low enough to make the deal a conservative moneymaker for you.

That said, investors all have a few dogs in their buying past. The key is to lose *little* when you lose, to win *big* when you win, and to make sure you win a lot more than you lose.   ■

The best way to tap into these deals is to hook up with a real estate agent in your area who specializes in these types of programs. If you ask around, you'll have no problem finding an agent to work with. It's up to you to train this agent about the criteria you have for the properties you want to buy. If you neglect to do this, your agent will show you every house on the multiple-listing service (MLS)—the proprietary database of properties for sale in an area. You don't have time to sort through all these properties.

That's one of the reasons your agent makes a commission—by helping you narrow the search for properties.

Also, be sure to make your own decisions on what price to offer. Many agents will say you can't offer such a low price and that you're crazy to try it. That's easy for them to say; not only do they have nothing to lose in the deal, but they also make more money on the higher price you offer. (Do you recognize a conflict of interest?) Instead, use your agent to help you find the houses you want to make offers on, to help write up and present your offers, and to help you do the paperwork once your offer is accepted. Be certain to do your own negotiating, and never tell your agent how much you're actually willing to pay. Even agents with the best of intentions can inadvertently cost you thousands of dollars.

ONE FINAL STRATEGY TO STRUCTURE THE DEAL

If you have decent credit and income to buy a foreclosure property at a good cash price, rather than take over the house "subject to" the existing financing, you could formally assume the financing that underlies the deal. We don't recommend it because you're much better off buying "subject to" the existing financing. Still, it's an option you should keep in your toolbox. If you decide to assume the loan formally, take into account the downsides (compared to buying "subject to"). To summarize, the disadvantages are as follows:

- *Increased risk.* The lender will make you sign personally on the loan.
- *Need for good credit and verifiable income.* The lender will make you fill out all the normal loan application documents you prefer to avoid.
- *Higher costs.* The lender will charge assumption costs ranging from $500 to a few thousand dollars.

FIGURE 3.5 *Calculating Costs*

Purchase and closing costs	❑ Purchase price	
	❑ Closing costs	
	❑ Title insurance	
	❑ Legal fees	
	❑ Document prep fees	
Lender's fees	❑ Appraisal	
	❑ Points	
	❑ Prepayment penalty minimum interest	
Fix-up and rehab costs	❑ Contractors	
	❑ Materials	
	❑ Temp Labor	
	❑ Permits	
	❑ Equipment rental or depreciation	
Holding costs	❑ _____ Monthly interest payments	
	❑ Electric	
	❑ Gas	
	❑ Water	
	❑ Sewer	
	❑ Insurance	
Selling costs	❑ Final cleaning	
	❑ Ongoing cleaning	
	❑ Advertising	
	❑ Signs	
	❑ Marketing assistant	
	❑ Commissions	
	❑ Concessions to buyer	
Value as confirmed by comps: _____	Total Real Cost	
Fast cash target – Flipping Value × .70 = _____ Fast cash target – Retailing Value × .90 = _____		
	Less Total Real Cost	
	Estimated Profits	

FIGURE 3.6 *Calculating Value*

24 percent is how much each **full bath** adds to the selling price of a house, making the bathroom the greatest value enhancer. Other impacts according to a recent study by Florida State University:
- Garage—adds 13 percent
- Air-conditioning—12 percent
- Fireplace—12 percent
- Basement—9 percent
- Bedrooms—each adds 4 percent

From *The Rocky Mountain News* 01/03/04

You just learned 12 powerful strategies to structure your fore-closure deals no matter the size of your bank account or the quality of your credit. (See Figure 3.7 for a review list.) Remember to consider all seven sources of funding the next time you negotiate a deal. Develop the confidence to know that if the deal is good enough, you'll always be able to fund it in some way.

You're better off to work only with sellers who are motivated to sell fast. In the next chapter, you'll learn 22 techniques to find motivated sellers.

FIGURE 3.7 *Review List of All 12 Buying Strategies*

"Subject to" financing

Short-term "subject to" financing when rehabbing

Wholesaling or flipping

Short sales

"Subject to" financing with discounting of debt

Funding source: seller

Funding source: your buyer

Funding source: your money or lines of credit

Funding source: private lenders

Funding source: money partners

Funding source: hard moneylenders

Funding source: VA and HUD financing

4

HOW TO INVEST IN THE CHANGING MARKET CONDITIONS WE ALL FACE

We've all noticed changes in the real estate landscape over the last few years. Recently, newspaper headlines shout out changes such as the following:

- "Are higher interest rates driving down the price of real estate?"
- "Home prices soften as market drops!"
- "Lenders flooding the market with foreclosure properties!"

Are the recent "boom times" in real estate investing really gone forever? The answer depends on your real estate expectations. Real estate—especially foreclosure real estate—has always been a good investment for conservative investors. (Most of us in The Mentor Family are quite conservative with our own investing, by the way.)

A conservative investor always does the following:

- Ensures that each property can pay for itself (see Chapter 9 for more on this)
- Avoids situations where the property *must* appreciate quickly for the deal to work
- Is cautious about investing hard-earned capital or personally signing on loans
- Tends to have a long-term mentality rather than a "get rich quick" mentality

Don't get the wrong message here. You can achieve vast sums of wealth with real estate. But if you expect it to come overnight and without a lot of hard work, you are fooling yourself.

TWO KEYS TO PROFITING IN ANY TYPE OF MARKET

Following are descriptions of the two essentials of making a profit in any real estate market.

1. Make Sure You're Buying with the Right Terms

The "right terms" means that you could, if needed, keep the property in your portfolio for six to eight years if either market conditions or a change in your plans requires it.

To do this, make sure that the property is able to pay for itself by bringing in rent or purchase payments that are higher than your total monthly costs. If the property can't pay for itself, pass on the deal. Too many profitable deals exist for you to waste your time on something that doesn't make money every month. You also need to master negotiating favorable, long-term financing. (See Chapter 5 for more on the Instant Offer System.)

Long-term financing is important in case you need to hold on to the property until your market bounces back. Real estate has increased in value at an average annual rate of 6.58 percent for the last 50 years. Remember, that's an *average*. Sometimes real estate prices soar, other times they go down or flatten out. As long as you are investing conservatively, market fluctuations won't be an issue for you.

2. Make Sure You Are Buying at the Right Price

You can realize quick cash profits by wholesaling foreclosures to other investors. (See Chapter 7 for more information.) The secret to selling quickly is making sure that you buy low enough for the next person to make a profit. Normally this means that you are buying at about 50 percent to 60 percent of market value and selling quickly at 65 percent to 70 percent of value. In a softening market, you'll need to remind yourself at the time of the sale that you bought the property for 60 percent or less of its value. If you are rehabbing (another reason we don't like rehabs), this could be six to eight months down the road. Even on a quick flip deal, by the time you first look at the property, close on it, and sell it, three or four months could pass.

Let's look at a marginal deal—a property you bought at 65 percent of its value. If the real market value softens by 5 percent and you have to allow another 5 percent to move the property due to "investor uncertainty," you might lose some money or, at best, break even.

 ■ **Success Team—Commercial Coach Stephen's Story**
At this point in my career, I pass on marginal deals. I've wasted lots of time on deals that didn't have enough of a profit spread to make them worth my time. With the same amount of time and energy, I could have found three or four deals with a profit of $20,000 or more. Don't be fooled into thinking you can make a bad deal better just by working on it harder. The largest profits are

made when you buy; the next largest profits are made when you sell. Trying to make a marginal deal better between buying it and selling it is a waste of time.

The secret to buying right is finding motivated sellers. As the market levels off, this is easier to do.   ■

WHO ARE MOTIVATED SELLERS AND HOW CAN YOU FIND THEM?

We are often asked, "If I live in a nice area, are there motivated sellers in my neighborhood going through foreclosure?" The answer is yes, there are foreclosures in your neighborhood. Statistics indicate that nationally, an average of 44 houses out of 1,000 are in foreclosure. People in your neighborhood are going into foreclosure.

Every day, hundreds of properties are bought and sold in your area. Some of these are creative transactions, and others are foreclosure properties. While most are more traditional deals, we haven't found an area yet where the system doesn't work. I think that's because this is really a people business. Once you learn how to connect with motivated sellers, you'll discover that people are pretty much the same no matter what market you are investing in.

But the real question isn't, "Are there foreclosures in my area?" but rather, "Where should I invest if I'm targeting foreclosure properties?" Every town has a variety of areas. There are nice areas of town where the residents live in big houses and drive nice cars. They have good jobs. They are doctors, lawyers, or business owners.

There are middle-class areas. Generally, in working-class neighborhoods, you'll find everything from hourly wage earners to well-paid white-collar workers. Your town also has less desirable areas. People with jobs live there, too. Why is knowing all this important? Because no matter where they live, all of these people have things in common. They are all human beings. The vast majority of them work, and many are married and have families. What does this mean for the foreclosure market? Read on.

WHY PEOPLE PROBLEMS CAUSE PROPERTY PROBLEMS

What is it that you're looking for? You are looking for a property that is behind in payments. Notice I said a *property* is behind in the payments. You never want to risk making a seller feel embarrassed about missing mortgage payments. For this reason, when talking with a seller, always refer to the *house* being behind in payments. Often, mortgage payments are missed as the result of life-changing events. Causes vary, but the five most common reasons that a house gets behind on payments are as follows:

1. Relocation
2. Divorce or relationship problems
3. Financial difficulties
4. Tenant issues
5. Probate

Understanding these common causes for missing mortgage payments offers insights into how and where to find motivated sellers. Let's take a closer at the five causes.

Relocation

We live in a mobile society. Following are just a few reasons why people move:

- Jobs (promotion or new job)
- Marriage
- Family demands
- Retirement

If the reason for moving is job related, the sellers travel to the new location, look at schools, check out the neighborhoods, and purchase a new house. However, the current property hasn't sold yet. When sellers are moving and can't sell the house, they are faced with potential double payments or with the prospect of managing the property as a long-distance rental.

A similar situation occurs when two people who each own a home get married. One of the houses will need to be sold or rented. Or a retired couple may decide to escape the cold by moving to Arizona or Florida. If they can't sell their existing home, they are faced with the prospect of making two mortgage payments—a task made more difficult on a fixed retirement income.

Any number of situations could easily lead to having two mortgage payments. And if there are circumstances that make the property hard to sell—a soft market, a house in need of repair, not enough time to list with a real estate agent—the situation can be dire. That sets the stage for you, the investor, to come in and help a seller.

Divorce or Relationship Problems

Often when a married couple, or other people who are in a committed relationship, decide to call it quits, a nice home comes on the market for quick sale. The end of a relationship results in the need to sell a property because

- the house is too expensive for one person to maintain,
- the property is an asset that must be divided, or
- sellers want to make a clean break and a fresh start.

These sellers, working to put their lives back together and move on, may need your help to get out from under their property.

Financial Difficulties

Debt and money concerns are a reality for many sellers. Given the choice between foreclosure and selling, many owners choose to sell. Homeowners behind on their mortgage payments need your help. They could be a month or two behind, or they could be facing immediate foreclosure.

Tenant Issues

Landlords who want out are highly motivated sellers. Following are three reasons for this:

1. Since they don't live in the property, they don't need to find another place to live.
2. They are willing to wait for their equity as long as they can see it is a good investment.
3. Because the property is a rental and not their primary residence, chances are they won't need their equity immediately to purchase another property.

Probate

This is an untapped market for investors. Homes go into probate when a person dies and leaves a house to heirs, usually relatives. Many people who inherit property just want to sell it. If they can't sell it themselves, they might be attracted to your creative offer. Many people who inherit a property are willing to take a lot less for it than it is actually worth. After all, it was given to them. This creates a great opportunity to purchase properties for cash. It's not uncommon for the properties to show poorly because they need repairs or are outdated. If there was a mortgage on the property, there might be payments due.

■ Success Team—Peter's Story

After a long negotiation, I just bought a property as part of a probate sale. After I bought it, I talked with another investor who had tried to buy this same house for two years without success. The probate attorney was motivated because he needed to close out the estate. However, because this was a nice waterfront location, the heir who was living in the house didn't want the sale to go through. He made it hard to sell by doing things like refusing to show the property.

During the negotiations, having the support of the Mentor Family and being able to follow a system is what helped me to acquire it. After we've fixed it up, this one house will be worth at least $500,000 more than we paid for it. The lesson is to listen to your team even when you think your deal isn't going to work out. ■

We've discussed what motivates sellers and what to keep in mind when talking with them. But which area in your town should you target? Any area where you find the five circumstances previously listed. Again, the five are as follows:

1. Relocation
2. Divorce and relationship problems
3. Financial difficulties
4. Tenant issues
5. Probate

Make sure you take advantage of the recent market changes that have lead to an increase in foreclosures. And remember the following three rules:

1. Stay conservative by keeping a long-term mindset.
2. In quick cash deals, make sure you are buying right.
3. People problems cause property problems.

5

THE INSTANT OFFER SYSTEM—5 SIMPLE STEPS TO YES

Imagine you've worked hard to find sellers in default who sound motivated over the phone. You've passed through your initial phone qualification, and the financial details all look good.

You've spent a total of four hours finding this one seller and setting up an appointment to meet at the house to talk about buying it. You feel a bit nervous, but you put that aside and focus on the excitement of potentially signing up your first, or next, deal.

Fast-forward to your arrival at the seller's house. You pull up and park on the street in front of the house. You get your first real look at the house from the street and think it looks just like a normal house. No one would ever be able to tell by looking at the house from the curb that the seller is five payments behind and on the verge of losing it.

You step out of your car and walk up to the front door. At this point, all the "cool" you felt anticipating this meeting disappears. Your heart is racing like a runaway stallion. It's all you can do to keep yourself from turning around, getting back in your car, and driving away. "What am I going to say to the seller? What are my first words exactly? What questions should I ask? In what order? How should I say them? How will I know what to offer the seller?"

Have we got your attention now?

We're about to give you the road map—your step-by-step guide—to the answers to all these questions and more. You'll learn exactly how to handle a meeting with a seller in default—every time.

Those who have read our other books or purchased one of our advanced home study courses may have already learned about the negotiating strategies and techniques we are about to share with you. At the heart of these negotiating techniques is the five-step process we've developed and refined over the past 10 years. We call it the Instant Offer System, or IOS for short.

THE BIG PICTURE OF THE INSTANT OFFER SYSTEM

What comes next is a distillation of our best negotiating secrets as they directly apply to buying foreclosures. When you finish working with this section, you'll know what to say and in what order so you have the best chance to close the deal.

The Instant Offer System (IOS) is made up of five distinct steps that must happen in the correct order to get the seller emotionally and intellectually ready to sign the deal on the spot. The words *on the spot* tell it all. You'll always have the best chance to put a deal together if you get it signed at your first meeting with the seller. To do this, spend the time talking with the seller and helping him or her emotionally and intellectually process what you're offering.

Don't be fooled by the simplicity of this system. The IOS is simple, but it works in any real estate negotiation. We've used it to negotiate everything from the purchase of single-family homes to complicated, multimillion-dollar commercial real estate transactions.

Following are the five steps:

1. Connect with the seller
2. Set up an "up-front agreement"
3. Build the seller's motivation
4. Talk about the money
5. Take the "what if" step

Let's go through each of these steps in detail so that when you're finished reading (and rereading) this section, you'll have all the tools you need to go out and negotiate a moneymaking deal on your own.

STEP ONE: CONNECT WITH THE SELLER

Start by building rapport with the seller. Imagine you were a seller and you were in a financially vulnerable position. How would you feel about some "investor" coming over to talk about buying your house?

Can you imagine how cautious and guarded you'd be? How closed emotionally you might be? Your job is to take the first 5 to 10 minutes to establish a connection and affinity with the sellers.

How do you do that? You gently ask the sellers questions about themselves and their lives, building bridges wherever you genuinely can. The fact is that people like people who are just like them. So as you go through Step One, you'll draw sellers out of their shells and get them to talk candidly. Wherever possible, you'll highlight when you're just like they are.

Here's an example of how this conversation might go. Imagine you, the investor, are walking through the house and the seller is showing you around:

Investor: Are these your kids? [*You point to the photo on the end table*]

Samantha: Yes, they are. That's Mark, my oldest, Sylvia, and Jonathon.

Investor: How old are they now?

Samantha: Mark's 26, Sylvia's 16, and Jonathon's 12.

Investor: My kids are 12 and 14 [*building a bridge*]. So does it get any easier when they hit their twenties? [*smiling*]

Samantha: It sure does. You know, I always thought it was real important to remember that we were all teenagers once and we survived it. Although looking back, I'm not sure how my parents survived my teen years. [*Notice how the seller is loosening up a bit.*]

Investor: I know exactly what you mean. I think I was probably the toughest of the bunch for my parents to raise [*building a bridge*]. What's your oldest doing now?

Samantha: He's married with a child on the way. He lives in Seattle and works for a financial company out there.

Investor: Wow, you're going to have a grandchild! That must be so exciting for you. How much longer until the due date? . . .

You get the idea; the first step of the IOS is to make a friend. We know some people will complain that they can't build rapport with the seller because they feel awkward and don't know what to ask. So here's a list of surefire questions to ask sellers. The following will jump-start the conversation if you ever feel stuck:

• Where did you grow up?
• Do you have any kids?
• How old are they?
• What do you do for a living?
• How did you get started in that career?
• What do you like to do for fun?

How to Avoid the Two Biggest Mistakes When Building Rapport

When trying to build rapport, it is essential to avoid the following two mistakes:

1. *Mistake 1: Spending too much time on rapport (not moving to Step Two fast enough).* At some point, a beginning investor wastes hours of time making friends with a seller who just isn't in a position to sell the house. The investor spends so much time building rapport that by the time he or she determines that the property obviously isn't a fit, the investor has wasted several hours of precious time.

   What do you really think causes an investor to remain in Step One of the IOS and not move on? If you said *fear*, you're right. The ideal amount of time to spend building rapport during Step One is 5 to 10 minutes.

2. *Mistake 2: Thinking that Step One of the IOS is done just once, ticked off, and forgotten.* Building rapport with the seller is something you'll have to do throughout your meeting. While you should spend only 5 to 10 minutes before moving on to Step Two (setting an up-front agreement), that doesn't mean you're finished building rapport.

   Throughout your negotiation, you will have to gauge your connection with the seller and look for opportunities to broaden and deepen this connection. But you have to balance this need to maintain the connection with your equally important need to move the conversation forward.

STEP TWO: SET AN UP-FRONT AGREEMENT

What is your most precious resource as an investor? Some people will say money. Others will say good credit. We say it's time.

Yet we watch so many beginning investors work for *free!* By this, we mean they invest all kinds of time and energy before they have a definite commitment from the seller that they have reached an agreement.

We're not willing to work for free, and we don't think you should, either. Instead, make it understood up front that you'll spend the time it takes to work through the situation and the details, provided the seller agrees early in the conversation that when it's over, both of you will let each other know exactly where you stand—either you have a fit or you don't. Period. It's that simple. In its plainest terms, an up-front agreement is simply a commitment from you and the seller to say *yes* or *no* at the end of your conversation about the property.

The following dialogue illustrates how it goes:

Investor: Samantha, I'm willing to sit and invest the time to listen to all the details of your situation and to talk through all the possible options we can come up with. All I ask is that when we're done talking this through, if what we talk through obviously isn't a fit for you, that you be willing to let me know. If it just isn't a fit, are you willing to tell me that?

Samantha: Sure.

Investor: I appreciate that. I'm letting you know that you're not going to hurt my feelings. On the other hand, if what we talk through *is* a fit for you, are you willing to let me know that when we're done here today?

Samantha: Yes, if it's a fit, I can tell you that.

Investor: Now I'll be doing the same thing in reverse. If I can't see a way where I can meet your needs and make a profit for myself, then I'm not going to want to buy your house. Are you OK if I have to tell you no, I don't want to buy it? I mean, it wouldn't be anything personal about you; it would just be me saying it's not a fit.

Samantha: I understand this has to work for both of us.

Investor: Exactly, and if I feel it's a fit, then I'll let you know that, too. I'll say, "Samantha, this is a fit for me, too." So what we're agreeing to do up front is to let each other know when we're done exactly where we stand. Either *no, it's absolutely not a fit.* Or *yes, it is a fit.* Is that what we just agreed to do? [*This is called "reinforcing" the up-front agreement.*]

Samantha: Yes it is . . . [*and on to the next step*].

Do you see how powerful that language and strategy is? It's your way of telling sellers that you'll put your time in to see if it's a fit, *if and only if* they'll promise to give you a decision right at the end.

■ **Success Team—Coach Juli's Story**

A time will come when you're scared to set a firm up-front agreement. When that moment comes, remember that I coached you to do it anyway. Oh, you'll think the language will sound stilted and strange, but do it anyway. Then, in the closing moves of your negotiation, if you need to, gently but firmly remind the seller of your mutual commitment up front to make a decision. You'll find this clear stance helps liberate you from wondering what's going to happen next. Honor this agreement, and hold the seller to it, too. ■

STEP THREE: BUILD THE SELLER'S MOTIVATION

At this point, you've set the stage to begin your negotiation in earnest. You've connected with the seller, built rapport, and set your up-front agreement (by which the seller has agreed to give you a decision at the end of your negotiation).

Now it's time to move to the next step, which is negotiating with the seller on an emotional level. In this step, you help the seller connect with all the pressing reasons to sell and why you are the best option. We call this "building the seller's motivation."

■ **Success Team—Coach Robb's Story**

When you want to build a seller's motivation, think about how great athletes perform. They first carefully warm up and stretch before they go out and compete. They know that if they start without this preparation, they might pull a muscle or otherwise injure themselves.

It's the same with sellers. You need to help them warm up to the idea of selling to you at a price and terms that allow you to make a conservative profit. In the motivation step, you're helping them stretch and warm up to find a fit for both of you.   ■

A key outcome to be reached in Step Three is to help sellers break out of the denial they may be living in. So many sellers who are in foreclosure have deluded themselves into believing that it's not really happening. They rationalize away their situation or, even worse, block it out completely. Unless you are able to help them work through any barriers and be emotionally present with the consequences they might face from their situation, you'll be hard-pressed to both help the seller and get a great buy on the property.

One of the things we covered in *Making Big Money Investing in Real Estate Without Tenants, Banks, or Rehab Projects* was something called "negative phrasing." This one idea will turn upside down many of the traditional notions of negotiating with a seller.

When sellers are in foreclosure, they are scared some investor will come in and steal their house. And when people are motivated by fear, they look for what is wrong because they feel that if they can spot what's wrong, they can protect themselves. Sellers who are motivated by fear will "mismatch," meaning they'll look for what's wrong. This is a term from Neuro-Linguistic Programming (NLP) that refers to a person's tendency to see and say the opposite of what he's told. For example, if you say to the seller that he'll never get the price he wants, he'll be even more convinced that he will. If you say that the condition of the house isn't good, she'll argue that it is good.

This is a leverage point for you in negotiations. *Whenever you can accurately predict how the other person in a negotiation will behave, you can use this information to be more effective.*

Following are a few simple examples of how to use negative phrasing to build the seller's motivation.

Example one:

Investor: You mentioned that you thought about refinancing as a way out. The mortgage brokers you talked with probably have already got that process going, right?

Seller: Well, actually, the guy I talked with said with my credit, I wouldn't be able to refinance the house.

Example two:

Investor: How else have you tried to sell the house?

Seller: We've been selling it "for sale by owner" for the last few weeks.

Investor: And that's been working really well for you?

Seller: Actually, it hasn't been working at all.

Example three:

Investor: You told me on the phone that you met yesterday with another investor. How did that go? I mean you probably really connected with him, huh?

Seller: Not really. He was a bit rude and pushy, and I ended up asking him to leave.

Do you get the idea? Rather than coming out and saying what you mean directly, you simply say the opposite and let the seller step into the powerful role of the one getting to correct you. This is one important reason that negative phrasing works so well when negotiating with sellers in default. Considering how powerless many sellers in their situations feel, you can probably see how by giving them the emotional currency of feeling powerful, you can really draw them out of their shell and connect emotionally with them. Also, notice how you are getting the seller to be the one who argues for your case, that he really is in trouble and does need your help. After all, whom is the seller more likely to believe, herself or you?

Remember, sellers who are in foreclosure are embarrassed to admit their situation, even to themselves, so they live in denial. That is why it's so important to spend the time with them to build their motivation. We mentioned that Step One (connecting with the seller) of the IOS should take 5 to 10 minutes; Step Three (building motivation) should take you closer to 30 minutes—the longer the better.

 ■ **Success Team—Commercial Coach Stephen's Story**

Every time I watch Peter negotiate on a property, I am still awed. Over the years, I've modeled his incredible ability to help sellers get in touch with the real reasons they need to sell fast. He's so good at it. That's one of the reasons why our IOS of today is vastly better than it was 10 years ago—because The Mentor Team (including me) has modeled all the powerful improvements Peter has come up with over the years.

When people ask me how I got to be so good at negotiating and investing, I explain how Peter invited me to become one of his Mentorship students and went on to help me become a Level Three investor. I made my first million by age 43 starting out with little knowledge of real estate investing. I accomplished that in less than two years of becoming a full-time investor.   ■

What follows is a sample of a transcript of an actual negotiation:

Investor: So, Samantha, you were telling me on the phone a few days ago that you had just received a letter from your lender saying it was about to start the official foreclosure. A lot of people would be scared by that kind of letter, but you probably just took that in stride, right? [*Negative phrasing*]

Samantha: Not really; it freaked me out. I mean it was really scary to get that letter.

Investor: Oh, really . . . tell me more about what you felt when you got that letter . . . [*voice dropping lower in tone and softer in volume*].

Samantha: I remember thinking to myself, "What am I going to tell my family if I lose the house?"

Investor: I imagine that must have been hard for you to think about. I know a lot of people would just run away and hide from the truth. Heck, you were probably tempted to just run away from what that letter meant. [*Negative phrasing*]

Samantha: No, I knew I couldn't run away. I mean, sure I thought about it for a moment, I still do at times, but I know that isn't going to help any.

Investor: Well, if worst came to worst and you lost the house to the bank, I'm sure your family would be supportive and wouldn't judge you in any way. [*Negative phrasing said with big eyes*]

Samantha: They'd be there for me, but they sure would let me know how I had messed up.

Investor: How do you mean? [*Scrunchy face, voice getting softer*]

Samantha: They'd make comments and whatnot. It wouldn't be too obvious, but they would take little shots and stuff like that. I don't want to have to deal with that when I'm back visiting for the next 10 or 20 years . . .

And the conversation would continue on along those lines. Go back and read through the sample transcript one more time. This time, look for other techniques used in this negotiation to help the seller emotionally associate closely with the situation instead of holding it at a distance. (Hint: We did this when we asked questions like, "Tell me, what did you feel when you got that letter?" and "How do you mean?")

You're giving the seller prompts so he or she goes into more detail about how the situation feels. This scares a lot of investors. They say, "I wanted to buy foreclosures because I like houses, or because I like running numbers, not to have some kind of touchy-feely conversation with a seller." The truth is that "houses and numbers" are not the business you're in. *Connecting emotionally with sellers who need your help is your core business.* Never forget this.

One of the greatest skills you can develop is your capacity to be comfortable guiding other people through tough emotional experiences.

STEP FOUR: TALK ABOUT THE MONEY

Now you are ready to talk through the numbers with the seller. Notice that you need to save this part of the negotiation for near the end. One of the biggest mistakes we see investors make is to negotiate the numbers—the money—without building the seller's motivation first. This can cost you tens of thousands of dollars on every deal.

■ **Success Team—Coach Emily's Story**

Class after class, our Mentorship students find that the Nothing Down Game™ they play at our three-day Intensive Training is the most powerful part of the training. Not only do they get to role-play the whole IOS, but they have defined criteria to help them make sure they stay on track. One of the most important ways they keep from getting penalty points (and are more likely to be able to "keep" their deals) is to always cover motivation before money.   ■

Remember this the next time you negotiate on a house: the seller will do his or her best to push you to talk about the money early in the negotiation. No matter how temptingly the seller brings up the subject of money early in the negotiation, keep firm and fully cover the seller's motivation before you move on to discuss money. You'll always get a much better deal this way.

There are two goals for the Money Step: first, to get all the sellers' financial details on the table; second, to gather all this information and *at the same time*, lower the sellers' expectations about the amount of money they'll receive and when they'll receive it. You might be thinking that you could never do both of these things. But we believe that anyone with a little coaching can become a great negotiator. Great negotiators are made, not born. Are you open to our coaching? We are about to give you the word-for-word language patterns that can lead to a slam-dunk when negotiating with sellers in default. Still, it's up to you to put them into practice.

> **INSIDER SECRET:** Learning to negotiate well is like learning a foreign language. The best way is to have plenty of repetition and immerse yourself in the sounds of native speakers. (That's why we recommend that clients who get our home study course listen to the negotiating sections over and over again.) At a certain point, you'll find yourself able to use just the right language, at the right moment, in the right way. It's similar to how you take in and learn lyrics to songs. After hearing the song over and over, one day you just know the words. It's effortless. As part of your Bonus Web Pack, you'll be able to listen in as The Mentor Success Team role-plays the entire Instant Offer System for you. (See Appendix A for details.)

The best way to learn how to negotiate money is to listen in to an actual negotiation, such as the following:

Investor: So what do you think the house is conservatively worth, Samantha?

Samantha: About $350,000.

Investor: Oh, it's worth conservatively $330,000 to $350,000, OK . . . [*Range technique—see our book* Making Big Money Investing in Real Estate *for this and 22 other powerhouse negotiating techniques.*]

Samantha: Actually, I think it's worth $350,000.

Investor: Oh, pardon me . . . $340,000 to $350,000.

Samantha: Yeah, I guess it's around there.

Investor: Let me ask you, what did you realistically think you would get, considering the house's situation?

Samantha: I thought I'd get at least $335,000 or more.

Investor: Oh, OK . . . you thought you'd get $320,000 to $335,000 . . . [*If the range technique works once, use it again!*] Let's see . . . a thought just occurred to me, if a real estate agent came to you and said he could get the house sold in the next 30 days, and you were convinced he could get it sold for you in the next 30 days for, let's say, the full $320,000 or maybe even a little bit more, you'd probably turn that offer down, huh? [*Negative phrasing*] Or maybe you wouldn't? You tell me. . . .

Samantha: At this point, I'd probably just take it to be done with all this mess.

Investor: That makes sense. Let's see, 6 percent of $320,000 is . . . 6 percent of 100,000 is $6,000, so we times that by three to get . . . $18,000, plus 6 percent of the $20,000 is about . . . what, $1,200. So I'm getting the full commission as roughly $20,000. Is that what you're getting?

Samantha: Yes, I'd get about $300,000 after all is said and done.

Investor: I think you're right. You'd walk away with the $300,000, less your share of the closing costs [*notice how you just slipped that one back into the conversation*]. What do you think the closing costs would be, Samantha? I had a real estate agent friend who told me that the costs usually are about 1 percent, so in this case that would be what, around $3,000 or so. Does that sound like about what you thought they would be?

Samantha: I hadn't really thought to add them in. But I guess you're right. Gosh, it doesn't really seem like I'd get much of anything. (Note: You haven't written any number down until you get to this bottom number of $297,000, which you write down and label as "full price amount to seller." Remember, in any negotiation, the person who is the one to label different pieces of information has a tremendous advantage.)

Investor: What was it you owe against the property?

Samantha: $280,000

Investor: Is that all on one first mortgage or spread between two or more loans?

Samantha: No, that's all on one first mortgage.

Investor: And the payment on that is . . .

Samantha: $2,350, and that includes the taxes and insurance.

Investor: And how many months is the house behind right now? [*Notice you said "the house," not "the seller."*]

Samantha: I'm four payments behind, going on five in two more weeks when the next payment is due.

Investor: Oh, so the house is about $10,000 behind as of the next payment, plus late fees and any other fees your lender tacks on . . .

STOP! You are done with Step Four of the IOS. You've gotten all the financial details down on paper in a way that has lowered the seller's expectation of what she will get. Now it's time to move on to Step Five—the "what if" step.

STEP FIVE: TAKE THE "WHAT IF" STEP

What if there was a powerful two-word phrase that would *guarantee* you'd never be rejected by a seller ever again? We're not saying it's possible, but again, what if it were possible that these two words would mean a seller would never reject any formal offer you made? If you could have these two words, what would it mean to you? How valuable would these words be to you in your investing? Would you be willing to donate $1,000 to your favorite charity just to get an email from us telling you what these two words were and exactly how to use them? You would? OK, we're a little confused here. Why would these words even be so important to you? All kidding aside, we hope you just noticed the language pattern of the preceding paragraph because it parallels exactly the tack you will take with the seller in this final step of the IOS. The two words that guarantee you'll never have a seller reject any formal offer you make are *what if.* These are the two most powerful words in any negotiation because they commit you to nothing, but they commit the other person to everything.

You can use these words effectively by qualifying any offer you choose to make to the seller with these two words. Then, before you "make" the offer, that person tells you that he or she would accept it. The words are so simple yet powerful that many would-be investors forget to use them when negotiating with a seller in foreclosure.

Here's a transcript of how those words might sound in action. We'll be building on our negotiation with Samantha. At its completion, we'll highlight several of the powerful techniques used in this transcript that you can immediately put to work to make your negotiations with any seller in foreclosure more profitable.

Investor: Samantha, here's an idea. You'll probably hate it [*negative phrasing*], but what if I were to make up the back payments and buy the property, and just take over the payments from here on out? I'm not sure if I'd be willing to do this or not just yet [*reluctant buyer*], but what if I were able to talk my partner [*higher authority*] into doing this? Is that something we should even talk about, or probably not? [*Negative phrasing*]

Samantha: No, I don't hate it. We should definitely talk about it.

Investor: Oh, OK . . . I'm a little confused here. I guess it's been a long day or something. What about me making up your back payments and buying the property, and then taking over your payments each month from here on out—would that even work for you? [*Scrunchy face*]

Samantha: Well, you'd stop the foreclosure so I wouldn't have that on my credit record for the next seven years.

Investor: Why's that even important to you?

Samantha: Because my credit is important to me. I mean, it affects my buying another house someday. It affects my car insurance costs. Besides, I just don't want to be the type of person who doesn't honor her obligations.

Investor: Oh, so if I'm hearing you right, you want me to make up your back payments, buy the property, and take over making the monthly payments from here on out [*giving the seller full credit for the idea*]. Did I get that right?

Samantha: Yes, that's what I want you to do.

By the way, if you liked the negotiating techniques you've learned about so far, make sure you get a copy of *Making Big Money Investing in Real Estate Without Tenants, Banks, and Rehab Projects* right away. We went to great lengths to build on the 23 negotiating techniques taught in that book. We know, you're thinking that you just spent $20 on this book; now these authors tell me to get their *other* book. Yes, that's exactly what we're saying. When you get it and read it cover to cover within 30 days of buying it, if you don't feel it's worth 10 times the price, we'll refund every penny you spent on it. This isn't the publisher talking; it's The Mentor Success Team guarantee.

It's that good. If you don't agree, just go to *www.ResultsNow.com* and send a quick note with your store receipt and the book. Tell us you want a refund and we'll send it, no questions asked. Do we have a deal? Heck, you probably hate that idea. [*Negative phrasing*]

HOW TO AVOID THE SEVEN BIGGEST NEGOTIATING MISTAKES MOST INVESTORS MAKE

You can avoid the seven biggest negotiating errors if you observe the advice described in the paragraphs below.

Mistake 1. Chasing the Deal

The best negotiators know that they can't appear to be too eager to make a deal. In the negotiating game, to be as effective as you want, you need to be a bit coy. Remember, reluctant buyers never chase after the deal; they seem hesitant, almost as if they are ready to walk away from the deal at any moment. This reluctance fuels the seller's desire to want the deal even more.

What follows are two quick examples of how reluctant buyers sound and the specific language patterns they use.

Example one:

Seller: What do you think you are willing to pay me for the house?

Investor: Well, Mr. Seller, to be frank, I'm still not sure I even want the house. What with all the craziness that is going on in the world today, I'm just not sure now is the time to pick up another investment property. May I ask you a few more questions to see if I even want to buy the house? [*Imagine you were the seller and heard such reluctant language. Can't you just feel your stomach sink?*]

Example two:

Investor: I'm not sure if I could even do this, but what if I was able to negotiate with your lender to have it accept a lot less money as full payment on what you owe? If I could do that, and I'm not sure I could, but if I could, would that be a fit for you, or probably not?

Seller: Yes, that would be a fit. Can you really do that?

Investor: Well, I'm not really sure I can, but I'll give it my best go. If I could, that would mean you could just walk away and start fresh somewhere else. . . .

Do you see the patterns of qualifying everything added into the negative phrasing? They work powerfully when combined like this.

Mistake 2. Selling the Seller on the Deal

Remember, when you are negotiating with a seller, you need to play the role of the reluctant buyer. So often we see other investors forget what they are doing and try to sell the seller on the deal. What this sounds like follows:

Average investor: Mr. Seller, what if I were able to buy your house for all cash at closing? This would give you immediate debt relief [*benefit one*], which would mean no more angry bank letters in the mail or bank bill collectors calling you up on the phone [*more benefits*]. Can you imagine how good that would feel to be free of this property?

You might be asking what's wrong with this dialogue. After all, "benefits sell" so why shouldn't you stack benefit on top of benefit to make your solution to the seller's problem even more appealing. All we can say is that it just isn't effective to sell the sellers on the deal. And this is especially true when the sellers are feeling vulnerable, as they surely must feel if they are in foreclosure. Following is what we anticipate would happen (the seller's response) when we continue the conversation:

> *Seller:* Well, I don't know. It all sounds good, but somehow it just sounds too easy. Besides, you'd never pay me enough to be something I'd accept. [*See how the seller is getting a bit nervous here.*]
>
> *Average investor:* I understand how you feel, Mr. Seller, but consider what it would really mean to you if we could get you the cash you need to just cut your ties to the house and get on with your life. We're talking all cash at closing. You do like the sound of all cash at closing, don't you?
>
> *Seller:* Of course, I like the sound of all cash, but it's just not going to work for me the way you describe it. I appreciate your time, but I just don't think we'll find a fit here.

And the more the average investor pushes the seller, the firmer the seller's stance becomes that there just isn't a fit. What the average investor didn't realize is that in *every* negotiation, there is always an eager party who wants the deal to close and a reluctant party who cares significantly less if the deal closes. The average investor mistakenly chose the wrong role!

Then the average investor compounds the error by trying to "convince" the seller. We've found that you can't convince motivated sellers of anything; you can only help lead them to the conclusions you want them to reach.

If we were negotiating this deal, we would use the following language to move the seller to the same conclusions that the average investor tried to jam down his throat:

> *Investor:* Mr. Seller, if I did decide to buy this house, which I'm not sure I want to yet, I probably would want to do it with an all-cash offer. But you probably want an offer where you

don't get all cash at closing but rather get paid payments over time, huh?

Seller: Actually, I prefer getting all cash at closing.

Investor: Really? Why would you want all cash at closing even though you know it will mean you get less for the house, because any investor would need to make a fair profit for even wanting to buy the place?

Seller: Because it would get me out from under all this debt and let me get a clean break.

Investor: What is important to you about getting out from under the debt and getting a clean break?

Seller: You don't know what it's been like for me and my family, what with all the nasty letters from the bank and the stress of not knowing what to do. I just want to be done with it, to cut my ties and get myself and my family a clean break from this house.

Do you see how a little more subtle approach is so much more effective because it harnesses the seller's natural tendency to be much more comfortable with the conclusions he makes compared to the facts and "benefits" you spoon-fed to try force him to agree with your conclusions?

Look for this *big* danger point when closing on the deal. Remember that during the "what if" step, the investor asks the sellers if that solution is something they should even talk about. When sellers say yes, most investors *blow it*. "How?" you ask. By getting all excited with the sellers' provisional yes and rushing into the opening with as many benefits as the investor can fit in, as quickly as possible. ("Oh great, Mr. and Mrs. Seller, this will really take the strain off you and your family and give you back your peace of mind. I bet that peace of mind is worth everything to you, huh?")

Mistake! Instead of rushing in like that, which only makes the sellers put up their guards and start to look for what's wrong

(What's wrong with this picture? What are we missing that makes this investor seem so eager here?), use a little negotiating leverage to get the sellers to close the deal themselves!

Following is a conversation showing exactly how to do this:

> *Investor:* What if I were to make up your back payments and buy the house? Then I'd take over your payments every month. I'm not sure at this point I'm even willing to do this, but what if I was willing to? Is that something we should even talk about, or you probably hate the idea, huh?
>
> *Seller:* No, I don't hate the idea.
>
> *Investor:* Oh, OK . . . What about my making up your back payments and taking over your payments? Is that a fit for you?

Do you see how you are getting the sellers to follow up with the benefits they get if they do business with you? The sellers are literally *selling themselves* on the benefits. And, of course, this is a thousand times more powerful than any benefits you could convince them of.

Tap into human nature in your negotiations to become even better at closing deals. Let the sellers sell themselves and you on the deal. Don't ram benefits down the sellers' throats; instead, let them tell you all the reasons why they think your offer is the right fit.

Mistake 3: Being the Ultimate Decision Maker

One important rule is: make sure those on the other side always have all their decision makers with them, while you always have a "higher authority" to appeal to elsewhere. This higher authority could be a partner or board of directors or spouse or attorney. While it might seem effective to be the one in charge—the decision maker—nothing could be further from the truth. Every investor needs a higher authority in all negotiations.

By using a higher authority, you are creating an environment in which you can accept concessions from the sellers but can't make certain concessions yourself. Or if you make these critical concessions, you get to qualify them with your need to get them past your partner, a higher authority. Also, this helps you maintain the position of the reluctant buyer who needs to be sold on buying the property.

Following is what this sounds like in a negotiation:

Investor: So if I'm hearing you right, you want us to get you $8,000 cash, plus make up your back payments and take over the monthly payments from here on out. Did I get that right?

Seller: Yes.

Investor: Are you sure that would even work for you? I mean, before I try to get my partner to go for this, I want to make certain that you are sure it is a total fit for you.

Seller: Yes, it's a fit for me.

Investor: And why was it again that you felt that this was a real fit?

Seller: Like I mentioned before, it gives me enough money to start fresh and to keep my credit intact.

Did you see how the use of the partner (*higher authority*) will allow you to get the seller to make a much firmer commitment that the deal is a fit?

Mistake 4. Taking Credit for the Solution

A pattern we've seen play out frequently is when one party receives the financial payoff while the other party gets the emotional payoff of being important and smart. We've also noticed that rarely will one person receive both payoffs. So what will it be for you? Are you willing to give the sellers the emotional and psychological payoff to make a healthy profit? Glad to hear it!

One of the most important ways to give sellers emotional currency is to give them 100 percent credit for the "solution" they come up with. Don't let your ego step in and claim ownership of the fancy solution *you* dreamed up. Be generous, making sure you compliment the sellers on their creative ideas.

What this sounds like in a real negotiation follows:

Investor: Let's see, when you added up all those estimated repairs we went through, what was the final amount you came up with?

Seller: $35,000.

Investor: OK, so let's see . . . the price you said you would take just to be done with the house, and which you felt the house would get if it were fixed up, was $340,000. Did I get that straight?

Seller: Yes, you have that right.

Investor: So let's see, after we factor in the repairs of $35,000 to get the house right to sell fast for the $340,000, and after we factor in the $5,000 in back payments, and the $270,000 that the bank is owed, you would get . . . $30,000. And your idea was for us to just get you your equity of $30,000 and you would deed the house over to us, is that right?

Seller: Yeah, I just want what's coming to me and then to walk.

Investor: Boy, I can sure understand that. An idea comes to mind, you'll probably think it's crazy, but what if we were willing to buy the property and make up the back payments, spend all the time and money to fix it up, and then sell it right away? And when we resell the property a few months from now, we'd get you a cashier's check for $30,000. The reason I even bring this up is that this way, we can keep the cash in the deal to around $40,000, which makes it much easier for me to convince my partner that this is a good deal for us. [*We couldn't resist throwing a little higher authority in for good measure.*] But you probably think this is crazy, that you'd rather just keep on selling it yourself, huh?

Seller: No, I don't think it's crazy. I can understand that you're trying to make this a good deal for you, too. How am I going to make sure I get paid my $30,000?

Investor: That's a really good point. I'm guessing that your idea was to make sure you secure yourself with the paperwork that requires us to pay you your money before we can sell the house to our buyer. That is important for you, and I'm glad you brought that up. I would have if I were you. Yeah, so we'll make sure we get a deed of trust in place to protect you just like you were the bank. Not to mention all the money that we're going to have to put in here to fix up the house before we resell it.

Seller: Good, I just wanted to make sure that I was covered.

Investor: Of course. Now, I just want to make sure I have it all clear. What you said you wanted us to do was to buy the house and make up the back payments, signing that deed of trust to require us to get you your $30,000 before we can sell it to our buyer, then we'll fix up the house and sell it as quickly as possible so we both get paid. Did I get what you had said right?

When it comes to spending psychological currency, don't be stingy! Give the seller credit wherever you can. Did you notice *five* specific places in the negotiating transcript where we gave the seller credit for coming up with a good idea or ownership of an answer in the negotiation that let the seller feel smart (one form of psychological payoff)? Go back over this conversation until you can spot all five instances of giving the seller psychological currency.

Mistake 5. Talking (and Thinking) Too Fast

Sometimes investors forget to play the "reluctant" role by talking too fast. This can really put the seller on guard and create a barrier to emotionally connecting with the seller.

Three quick techniques to make sure you don't fall victim to this pitfall follow:

1. *Slow down.* Always make sure your pace of speech is just a bit slower than that of the seller. People instinctively associate fast-talkers with wheeler-dealers and sharpie investors.
2. *Adopt a passive posture.* Round off your shoulders, let your stomach relax, lower your head. Why? Because alert, angular body posture and sharp, fast movements and gestures make it difficult for a seller to relax and feel comfortable being open with you. This also softens your voice and mutes the energy you send off, which in turn relaxes the seller even more.
3. *Special warning for men.* The two previous points are ten times more critical for you than for women. If you're negotiating with a woman, you have to put her at ease and not intimidate her. For example, this means being respectful by not standing or sitting too close to her and talking in a soft voice and manner. With other men, you'll have to be cautious not to butt heads. Let the man you're negotiating with feel physically comfortable by using the other two techniques. You'll negotiate a much more profitable deal by neutralizing the danger of getting into an ego battle.

Mistake 6. Not Letting the Seller Save Face by "Winning" at Parts of the Negotiation

In your negotiation, look for places where you can help sellers feel as though they've won. Sellers have to be able to face their families and neighbors, not to mention themselves. Help them be winners.

Mistake 7. Using Impressive Language That Intimidates the Seller

The final mistake is using jargon and technical language with the sellers. While it might feel good for you to use words such as *"subject to"* and *wholesaling* and *assigning*, we caution you about using them. Remember, in any negotiation there are two payoffs. Talking in impressive language will give you the psychological payoff, but it will often kill a deal. It makes sellers feel less intelligent, more confused, and more intimidated. Instead, always talk in descriptive language that immediately makes sense to the seller.

Following are two quick examples:

Example one:

Investor: What if we were to make up the back payments and buy the house? Then we'd just take over making the payment each month. Is this something we should even talk about, or you probably hate the idea, huh? [*You just offered to buy the house "subject to" the existing financing.*]

Example two:

Investor: Well, I'm not sure if this is even going to be a fit for me. I'm having a hard time imagining I could even get my partner to go along with this. But what if I could get my partner to agree to get you the $100,000 cash—would you be open to talking about waiting 60 to 120 days, maybe 180 days at the most, to get that $100,000? We'd need this time to complete the renovation on the property and find a buyer to get us both cashed out of the property. Should we even talk about this option, or probably not? [*You just offered to do a short-term "subject to" financing deal and cash out the seller by reselling the house to a retail cash buyer as soon as possible.*]

You now have a complete system for negotiating with sellers. This five-step framework took us years to create. All these ideas have been tested in the real world and have been proven to work, making investors like you a lot of money. Give yourself some time to integrate these negotiating ideas into your investing; return to this chapter again and again to refine your technique. The payoff is worth the investment you put in because negotiation is one of the most important investing skills you can ever develop.

C h a p t e r

6

24 FORECLOSURE PITFALLS THAT CAN COST YOU BIG!

This chapter shows you how to avoid the major pitfalls of buying from sellers in foreclosure. It draws heavily from deals done by the Mentor Family (especially the ones that went bad) so you can shortcut your learning curve. We learned about all 24 of these pitfalls the hard way; The Mentor Team shares them here to help you profit from our painful experiences.

PITFALL #1: LETTING THE SELLERS STAY IN THE HOUSE

At some point in your foreclosure career, probably on your first or second house, you are going to be tempted to let sellers stay in the property after you have purchased it. After all, they are in such a bad place and they have such a nice family and they only need a few weeks to find another place to move into. . . .

When that time comes, we urge you to come back to this section of the book and read the following words of advice. (As a matter of fact, put a note next to this section so that you can make it easier to find when you need it most.) Here is our advice: never, ever let the sellers stay in the property once you have purchased it.

Can we be serious? Deadly serious? If you let the sellers stay in the property, you're asking for trouble. Either they won't find another place, or they will keep coming up with reason after reason, excuse after excuse, story after story about why they need more time. And when you ask them to leave, they'll get angry with you, as if you were the one who caused them to stop making payments to their lender. All the while, if you're not careful, this situation will eat into your profits and potentially into your own checkbook. This point is so important, and so often ignored, that we've incorporated some subtle variations on this theme in the next pitfall.

PITFALL #2: RENTING THE PROPERTY BACK TO THE SELLERS

You will find many sellers who tell you they will sell you their house if only they can rent the property back from you. While they'll promise to take great care of the house and the numbers will look good on paper, don't do it!

We understand that it seems as if the deal won't work unless you give in on this point, but there is usually a better solution if you really put your collective minds to it. Blame it on your partner so you can still maintain your rapport with the sellers, but be very firm on this point—your partner won't let you buy the property unless the sellers move.

Just think for a moment. If the sellers can't make their house payments, how are they going to pay you rent? And if they don't pay you the rent and you move to evict them, just imagine the nightmare of having to deal with their getting more and more upset and rewriting the history of how you bought the property. The real history may have had you playing the role of hero, but we can guarantee you'll get cast in a more sinister role in this revised version. When the emotions get charged, usually the rational mind gets shut off.

■ Success Team—Peter's Story

I was in the process of buying a five-bedroom, three-bath house in my neighborhood that was in foreclosure. My real estate agent insisted on allowing the sellers to stay in the house after the closing. The sellers' agent promised that everything would be fine. Do you ever hear your gut talk to you? Even though my "gut check" said don't do it, I went along with letting the sellers stay in the house. A week later when we were supposed to have possession of the home, the sellers were gone, but two-thirds of their possessions were still in the house. When you get in a situation like this, you can't simply toss out the sellers' possessions because you may be liable for them. To make matters worse, in the sellers' minds, we had gone from being the "friendly investors" to somehow become the "greedy, impatient investors" who wanted the sellers out of the property. The best way to avoid this (and a variety of other possible complications) is to make vacating the property a condition of the sale no matter what.   ■

One "technique" used by some investors is to buy a foreclosure from a seller and rent it back to the seller with an option to buy the property back at a significantly higher price. The investor stops the foreclosure by making up the back payments. From the investor's perspective, theoretically either the seller exercises his or her option to buy back the property at a healthy profit to the investor, or the seller doesn't, in which case the investor keeps the house with its built-in profit. In most cases, the seller can't make the rent payments, and the investor has to evict the seller.

Not only do you have all the emotional hassles of this process, but you also have a lot of legal liability from the way the deal is structured. Technically in many states, the sellers could claim that you didn't buy the property from them but merely lent them the money they needed to stop the foreclosure. And because your "profit" (as built in by the much higher option price you gave back to them) could make your rate of return on the money you "lent" them by making up back payments higher than the state-allowed maximum, you could be guilty of usury.

As crazy as this may seem, this is a real possibility in many states. Our advice is to avoid structuring your deal this way. If, however, you want to do this, be sure to talk with an experienced real estate attorney about the legal implications in your county and state.

PITFALL #3: PUTTING *SERIOUS* MONEY INTO THE DEAL BEFORE THE SELLERS VACATE

We recommend that you never give sellers a large chunk of money before they have moved out of the property. This is your only real form of leverage to ensure that they do, in fact, live up to their word and move out.

Just what is serious money? This varies from investor to investor. Our definition of *serious money* is any amount of money that would cause you to pause before walking away from the deal. For some investors, this might be a few hundred dollars, for others a few thousand.

We also recommend that you hold up making all the back payments or investing serious money in the fix-up work until the sellers have moved out. If you do start investing heavily in the property, then with each dollar you spend, you become more committed to the deal. Then it becomes even harder for you to maintain the emotional detachment to deal intelligently with any risks that come when the sellers refuse to move out. The bottom line is that you only put serious money into properties that are keeper deals. And you only have a keeper deal if the sellers have moved out.

PITFALL #4: GIVING SELLERS ALL THEIR MONEY *BEFORE* THE FINAL WALK-THROUGH

Make sure you take the time to walk through the property before you hand over that final check to the sellers. Don't worry whether the property is clean or dirty; you are going to hire a professional cleaning service anyway. Instead, check for big things like damage to the property. Did the sellers leave the appliances (if that was part of the agreement)? You want to protect yourself from the shock of any unpleasant surprises.

■ Success Team—Coach Robb's Story
One of my friends, Rico, whom I've spent time with as part of The Mentor Family, told me about a house he recently bought along with his wife, Lynn. Because Rico started playing the piano a few years ago, they insisted the Steinway grand piano in the house be included in the deal. Rico and Lynn made sure to write it into the agreement. When Lynn flew out to the closing, The Mentor Team advised her to arrange for time to walk through the house the day before closing "just in case."

Rico got a call the day before closing from Lynn saying, "You'll never guess what's missing." The piano was gone. Because they had followed their Mentor's advice, Rico and Lynn got a credit for $35,000. They used it to remodel the home and substantially increase its value. Rico said that with the profits from selling the home, he'll be able to buy a brand-new Steinway and have enough left over to send his son through college.   ■

PITFALL #5: PUTTING SERIOUS MONEY IN THE DEAL BEFORE COMPLETING YOUR DUE DILIGENCE

The more money you have in a deal, the more you have to lose. Remember that any foreclosure deal may unravel after you conduct your due diligence. Make sure you haven't committed to the deal by putting in more money than you are comfortable walking away from.

In *Making Big Money Investing in Real Estate Without Tenants, Banks, or Rehab Projects*, we go into detail about the seven steps of your due diligence (pages 149–164). We encourage you to read through that section for a due diligence checklist and a step-by-step comprehensive guide. We share some insights that add to your due diligence in the next several pitfalls, which is especially important when you're buying foreclosures. Described below are two of them.

1. Talk with Neighbors to Get the *Real* Story

Often, neighbors are motivated to help you buy the property—they don't like the fact that their house is worth less because of the eyesore next door, or they're uncomfortable that the foreclosure situation will negatively impact their neighborhood.

They can often tell you the history of the house, any repair problems it's had, and much more. Some people hide information because they really want you to buy and fix up the property. But you'll find enough honest ones that, if you're a good listener, they'll tell you the inside story on the seller's situation and the history of the house. They can also give you valuable information on property values and trends, neighborhood concerns, and what's going on—good and bad—in the local area.

Carefully Read All the Seller's Loan Paperwork on Any "Subject to" Financing Deal

Always get copies of the actual loan documents from the seller. Read through these documents very carefully, especially the actual promissory note and deed of trust or mortgage. Sometimes sellers can mislead you about the terms or conditions of the loan. While rarely will they lie outright, many times they can be mistaken. If they don't have the paperwork anymore, contact their lender and have them fax or mail you a duplicate copy.

■ **Success Team—Peter's Story**

We bought a $125,000 house a few years back from a seller who just couldn't make the payments anymore. We made up five back payments and took over the property "subject to" the existing financing, which we thought was at a 7.9 percent fixed rate for 30 years. It turned out that the loan was an ARM—an adjustable rate mortgage. We got lucky because interest rates had dropped, but it could just have easily turned out the opposite, with interest rates climbing and the higher payment cutting into our positive cash flow. I know it's time consuming, but if you are buying "subject to" financing, take the time to look over the seller's loan documents. ■

PITFALL #6: NOT ACCURATELY DETERMINING THE REAL MARKET VALUE OF THE PROPERTY

Make sure you take the time to calculate conservatively the market value of the property. The two market values to check—the resale value and the market rental value—are discussed below.

1. Checking the "Comps"

It's important to know the market rental value of a property if you plan to sell it to an investor or if you plan to hang on to the property over time. Property values are determined for single-family houses by finding out what other similar (or comparable) houses in the area have sold for in the recent past. What this means is that a three-bedroom, two-bath, 1,850-square-foot house is probably worth what other comparable houses have sold for in a given area. Obviously, for two properties to be comparable, they need to have the following:

- Similar square footage (ideally within 200 square feet or less)
- Same number of bedrooms and bathrooms
- Similar construction type and condition, etc.
- Same school district and county

This is a simplification of the process of determining value. It takes time to learn how to value a home, and it's a skill you will learn. In the beginning, if you sign up a deal, latch onto a good real estate agent in the area who can help you determine its value. As a backup, you can always hire a professional appraiser for the first house or two you buy.

2. Checking Market Rents: Rent Survey

A *rent survey* is an analysis of rent rates for properties similar to the one you have under contract. While you might not be able to determine this value to the dollar, you almost always will be able to determine a range of rents. It's important for you to know the market rent value of a property, whether you plan to sell it to an investor or you plan to hold onto the property over time.

PITFALL #7: NOT CHECKING THE TITLE CAREFULLY ENOUGH

One of the biggest dangers in a foreclosure deal is that you aren't getting *marketable title* to the property you are buying. Marketable title means your ownership claim to the property is so strong that you can easily sell the property to a buyer who will bring in conventional financing, which requires a title insurance policy. The title must be free of any consequential clouds, whether they are actual or merely potential. That's just a fancy way of saying there can't be any liens or claims against the title that would scare a title company into listing these title glitches as "exemptions" to a title insurance policy. Otherwise, you will have significant trouble selling the property to a cash buyer. You'll learn more about title insurance in Pitfall #8. For the moment, you are going to have to get a title company to give you a title report, also known as an *ownership and encumbrance* report. This will show you all the liens against the property.

Checking Title Items

Following are 10 items to check when examining the chain of title:

1. County tax liens for nonpayment of property taxes
2. Homeowner association liens for fees owed or special assessments that are unpaid
3. Other taxing authorities' liens (city, state, or federal)
4. Mortgages (first, second, third, etc.)
5. Local utility company liens (e.g., for unpaid water and sewage bills)
6. Judgments from any creditors
7. Mechanics' liens

8. Other people on title (e.g., son or daughter listed on title as joint tenant)
9. Spouse or ex-spouse, including community property rights (more on this in Pitfall #11)
10. Heirs of the previous owner who might have a claim to the title

PITFALL #8: NOT BUYING TITLE INSURANCE IF YOU PUT SERIOUS MONEY IN THE DEAL

Title insurance protects you from any prior claim or cloud on the property title that happened *before* you bought it. This might be the only type of insurance that insures against past events. Basically, when you buy title insurance, you are paying the title company to research the chain of title thoroughly. The title insurance company issues a report that lists any "exclusions" to the policy. It's critical to check this part carefully. Make sure you're either comfortable with each item or you clear up any items in question before you close. If a claim arises that the title insurance company didn't list as an exclusion and it ends up costing you money later, the title insurance company will pay out money on that claim. As with any insurance, limitations exist, so have the title company explain them to you.

 ■ **Success Team—Coach Mike's Story**
When I put any real money into a property, I always buy title insurance. This might cost me several hundred dollars, but my peace of mind is more than worth it. I also recommend purchasing title insurance for all your foreclosure deals unless you're an experienced investor who's willing and able to intelligently take on the risk of not buying it.   ■

PITFALL #9: NOT RUNNING A CREDIT CHECK ON THE SELLER

Make sure you get sellers to sign a permission form to allow you to run a credit check on them. You'll need their Social Security numbers to run this credit report. Taking this extra step of running a credit check can save you a lot of heartache down the line.

What to Look For on the Seller's Credit Report

Look for the following essentials when checking the credit reports of sellers:

- Credit history that indicates a current or pending bankruptcy (see Pitfall #10)
- Marital status—important if you live in a community property state (see Pitfall #11)
- Any other creditors who may have claims to the property

PITFALL #10: SELLER DECLARING A BANKRUPTCY

A seller can file two types of bankruptcy:

1. Chapter 13 bankruptcy (restructuring) where the court imposes a forced payment plan on all creditors seeking payment
2. Chapter 7 Bankruptcy (absolving debts) where most types of debts are canceled

You are probably asking, "What happens if the seller declares bankruptcy? How does this affect the foreclosure process?" While many sellers think this will stop a foreclosure, they are wrong. The best sellers can hope for is a delay (typically a month or two) of the foreclosure until the lender petitions the court to release the property from the bankruptcy so that the lender can get on with the foreclosure process. The cost to the sellers is that their credit will be even worse with bankruptcy and foreclosure than with fore-closure only.

If the sellers have already declared bankruptcy before the sale, you will need the bankruptcy trustee's permission to allow the sale. This should not be a problem as long as the sellers aren't making a profit and you aren't getting too good of a deal. If you are, the trustee may feel that you are getting equity that should in all fairness go to creditors.

The biggest risk you have to protect yourself from if the seller declares bankruptcy is something called *fraudulent conveyance*. This is a legal term that means that the sellers didn't have the right to transfer the property to you because they were defrauding their creditors who rightfully should have gotten the equity in the prop-erty. This probably won't be an issue, as long as the sellers didn't have much equity. The sellers' creditors would actually have to file suit for fraudulent conveyance and prove that you knew of the sellers' debts and received too good of a deal in a way that wasn't fair to the creditors. If a court agrees with the fraudulent convey-ance claim, the sale can be set aside for up to two years. Our best advice is to make sure you talk with a highly skilled attorney if you are buying a property from sellers who either have declared or are about to declare a bankruptcy.

PITFALL #11: BUYING ONLY HALF A HOUSE

If you are investing in a community property state, then regardless of who is technically on the recorded deed, current or past spouses probably have an interest in that property. You'll have to protect yourself by getting both spouses to sign all important documents, such as the purchase contract and deed. Make sure that you get every signature notarized; sellers have been known to forge their ex-spouses' signatures. Check to make sure the notary lists *both* sellers' names on the acknowledgment and thus notarized both persons' identities and signatures, not only one signature (with the other signature forged later).

Another way to protect yourself is by getting a signed and notarized quitclaim deed from the other spouse or ex-spouse, deeding any interest he or she has in the property over to you. Or he or she can quitclaim his or her interest over to the spouse or ex-spouse, who then can sell you the property.

Community Property States

Following is a list of community property states:

- Arizona
- California
- Idaho
- Louisiana
- New Mexico
- Nevada
- Texas
- Washington
- Wisconsin

Also, ask a good attorney in your area about "palimony claims." Similar to community property claims, these arise when two people have lived together for so long that they may be regarded as a common-law married couple.

PITFALL #12: NOT GETTING THE PROPERTY PROFESSIONALLY INSPECTED

You need to know what you are getting yourself into. Hire a professional inspector and make sure you take the time to go over what the inspector has found so that you are making an intelligent decision about moving forward on the deal.

We don't recommend you act as your own inspector for two reasons. First, your time can be better spent by staying in the investor role, which is a more highly paid role than that of property inspector. Second, it's too easy in your excitement over what a great deal you are getting to overlook a problem that an objective inspector would catch.

PITFALL #13: MESSING UP YOUR PAPERWORK

While you will probably need legal help on your first few deals, fairly soon you'll be able to handle most of the closing paperwork yourself. Not only will this save you time and money, but it will also give you an extra degree of control in the closing process. Even if you use an outside escrow or title company to perform your real estate closings, by knowing how to prepare the documents yourself, you will be able to use these closing agents' services more intelligently.

Checking Your Paperwork

The three critical items to check on your paperwork are as follows:

1. *The owner's exact name and spelling on the title.* Make sure that the name on the deed and other paperwork is the same as the name on the deed through which the sellers gained title when they bought the property. If the owner is a corporation, limited liability company (LLC), or a trustee of a trust, make sure you see the written documentation that authorizes the seller to transfer title to you on behalf of this other entity.

2. *The correct legal description of the property.* This is the fancy "official" address used to identify the property accurately. It

usually looks like, "Lot 3, Block 5 of Sunny Side Acres Subdivision as recorded on Map No. 2377, page 744 as recorded . . ." You can copy this from the old deed or from the title report. Take care to get it right, or you will have problems later. We recommend you double-check it, then check it *backwards*—letter by letter, space by space—one time. Then have someone clse triple-check it, letter by letter, space by space.

3. *Use the right deed (or a deed normal for your area).* Get a copy of a deed from a local title company that your county's land records or recorder's office *is used to seeing.* You want the documents you plan on recording, like the deeds and Memorandum of Agreements, to be formatted just like the other documents that the recorder's office is used to seeing. This will help you avoid any title problems when you resell the property. Remember, to have marketable title, a title insurance company must be comfortable with the chain of title. If the deed you used to acquire title to the property is out of the ordinary, it will wave a red flag at the title insurance representative who is working on the title policy. You can easily avoid this by taking a little extra time to make sure your deeds and other recorded documents fit the format that is primarily used in your area.

PITFALL #14: NOT FOLLOWING YOUR STATE'S FORECLOSURE LAWS

Some states have specific laws about how investors must interact with sellers who are in foreclosure. Make sure you study the laws in your area so you follow them at all times. To save you many hours of research, we've included an overview here of many of the important laws in a number of states. In addition, you'll find an up-to-date state-by-state listing of laws affecting foreclosures in your Bonus Web Pack (see Appendix A for details).

California

For example, California is probably the toughest state for laws outlining what an investor can and cannot do. In California, anytime an investor buys a property from a seller who is in foreclosure (i.e., the notice of default has been filed), the investor must give the seller a five-day right of rescission. During this time, the investor is not allowed to get the seller to sign any type of deed or pay the seller any money. If the investor breaks these rules (or other rules of the state), then the sale can be turned aside at any point in the next two *years!*

Because of this, you are going to want to make sure you know and understand your state's laws that affect either the foreclosure process or your activities as an investor.

Colorado

Colorado has strict limits on *foreclosure consulting* services, which apply if you are offering to help owners stop foreclosure, repair their credit, assist by delaying the sale, or assist the homeowner in any manner other than an outright purchase.

When buying foreclosures in Colorado, know that there is a three-day right of rescission law along with requirements that your purchase agreements include the following:

- Full terms and details of any services the investor has provided before or after the sale
- Terms of any rental or lease with the homeowner
- Complete details of any option or ability for home owner to repurchase the home

We don't recommend allowing the homeowner to stay in the home or giving the owner any rights to repurchase the home. If you insist on doing this for some reason, make sure you and your attorney understand the strict limits imposed by reviewing the entire Colorado Senate Bill 06-071, which is available for you as part of your Bonus Web Pack (Appendix A).

Colorado law also requires that the investor does not make any statements that are misleading or untrue about the value of the home or the amount of money the owner may get from foreclosure. Finally, all contracts used to purchase homes in foreclosure in Colorado must include a version in the principal language spoken by the homeowner.

Texas

Texas has passed laws that restrict your ability as an investor to buy and sell property using *exculpatory contracts,* including land contracts and lease purchase agreements. This generally doesn't stop the foreclosure investor because we don't use these methods when focusing on foreclosure properties. Make sure you are actually getting title by buying "subject to" the existing financing or having the owner carry back the financing.

Another way to control a property without taking title or using a lease purchase is to get a sales agreement with an assignment clause and request a long time before the closing date or generous extensions for the closing date.

Because laws change, check with your own counsel no matter what state you are in to make sure you are meeting all of the requirements. (Your Bonus Web Pack in Appendix A includes a complete summary and links to Texas investing laws.)

Illinois

Illinois is similar to California in that contracts with homeowners in foreclosure must include the following:

- Five-day rescission period for the homeowner
- Disclosure of any services you are giving the homeowner before or after the deal
- Full terms of any agreement that allows the homeowner to stay in the home (We don't recommend this; see Pitfall #2.)

We've found that if you're putting together deals that allow the homeowner to feel whole, having a rescission period can actually work to your benefit by allowing the seller to get out of any deals made with other investors who don't invest the way we expect you to. (See your Bonus Web Pack in Appendix A or consult with your attorney for the latest updates on Illinois or other states that couldn't be included at press time.)

Maryland

When you are investing in foreclosures in Maryland, you must follow some specific guidelines, which include using a form required by the state. This form provides a detailed accounting of your net profits on the property, including a requirement that for properties resold within 18 months of purchase, 82 percent of the net profits must go to the seller. (We've included a copy of this form as part of your Bonus Web Pack in Appendix A.)

While this may seem like a major roadblock to investors, before you look outside of Maryland to other nearby states, understand that a restrictive law like this has two effects on investors. First, most investors simply throw up their hands and say, "I can't invest here anymore." Then a handful of investors find a way (e.g., they use a long-term holding strategy) to profit in a marketplace that suddenly has no competition. The secret is to learn the laws in your state and how to invest legally and ethically while staying within the limits of the laws.

PITFALL #15: FALLING INTO THE INSURANCE TRAP

The insurance trap comes in three varieties. First, many investors who buy a property, especially if they are buying the property "subject to" the existing financing, forget to convert the existing homeowner's policy into a landlord's or rental property policy. Not that we're cynical about insurance companies using any type of technicality to get out of paying out a large claim, but we advise you not to give them a chance. Make sure when the seller is endorsing over the existing insurance policy that you have the policy changed to reflect that it's no longer an owner-occupied property.

Second, don't forget to remove the seller's name from the policy. It would be a real shame if you filed a claim and simply because you didn't remove the seller's name from the policy, his or her name appeared on the claim check!

Third, when buying a property "subject to" the existing financing, it's tempting to take the seller's name from the policy and put in your name as the main insured party. The problem with this is that the existing mortgagee (the lender who lent the seller money to buy the property) is on the policy as the additionally insured party. As such, when the policy is changed in any way, this mortgagee will be notified. It doesn't take a rocket scientist at the bank to make the connection between there being a new main insured on the policy and the property being sold without the lender's permission. This could cause the lender to decide to exercise the due-on-sale clause.

As we shared with the readers of our last book, there are two ways to handle this. One is simply to leave the first insurance policy in the name of the seller and go out and get a second policy naming you as the main insured. Yes, this will mean paying twice for insurance, but the cost isn't that much compared to the benefit of getting the property "subject to" the existing financing.

The second way to sidestep this insurance trap is by using a *land trust*. A land trust is simply a trust that is created to hold title of a property for the benefit of some beneficial party. Any seller may put a property into a land trust without violating the due-on-sale clause, as long as the seller remains the beneficiary (by federal law.) Lenders are used to seeing this from time to time because some sellers will put their home into a trust as part of their estate planning.

To tweak this a bit to help you pay for just one insurance policy without providing false information to the lender, simply have the seller deed the property you are buying "subject to" the existing financing to a land trust. While the name of the land trust is recorded, the trust itself, which names you, the investor, as both the beneficiary and as the trustee, is not recorded. As long as you record only the deed showing the property going into the trust and not the trust document itself, the lender will typically leave you alone. Of course, if the lender calls you to ask you if you are the owner, you will let them know that yes, you do own the beneficial interest in the trust. Understanding that lenders really don't want to call loans due and being comfortable with the risks associated with this is essential for anyone who wants to use this strategy. We make sure that the lender gets a quick letter notifying it that the owner has put the property into a trust and, from here on out, all correspondence about the loan should be with the trustee (who happens to be you, the investor). You give the lender your address in this letter as the trustee, and from here on out, you will be the lender's contact person on the loan. (Note: Even though you know you'll always make the payments, you still have zero liability for this loan!) How does this help you with the insurance trap? You simply switch the policy from the seller to you as the trustee of the XYZ Property Trust. The lender expects and is used to this change.

Everyone is happy—the bank, the seller, the insurance company, and you the investor. This is our preferred way of handling "subject to" deals. Once you do one this way, you'll find it is fairly simple.

PITFALL #16: SELLER'S PUSHING THE LOAN TO GET CALLED DUE

While most sellers will respect their agreement to allow you to buy the property "subject to" the existing financing and not to do anything that would cause the lender to call the loan due, some sellers forget about their earlier promises. Several years later, they are no longer motivated sellers, and they really want you to get that loan out of their name, usually so they can more easily finance the purchase of another property. A few of these sellers will even take the next step—to force your hand by calling up their old lenders and telling them that they sold the house several years ago and that the lenders should call the loan due.

While you have no legal or financial obligation to pay off the loan if the lender does call it due, the lender could foreclose on the house, and you would then lose out on your equity. While this may seem scary, we want to reassure you that it isn't very likely. First, if you deal openly and intelligently with your seller up front, chances are very good that he or she will honor the agreement (more on this in a moment). Next, even if the lender does call the loan due, you can usually assume the loan, sell the property to a new buyer, or refinance the property. Typically, if you are polite and open with the lender, you'll have four to eight months or more to do this.

Five Ways to Protect Yourself from the Seller's Spilling the Beans

Following are five strategies to protect yourself from a seller's attempts to get the loan called due by the lender:

1. Make sure the sellers understand from the outset that if they intentionally cause the loan to be called due, it could be costly for both the sellers and the investor. Clearly state that the only reason this deal works for you as an investor is that the sellers allow you to bring the old loan current and take over the payments each month. Explain that if you had to bring in your own financing, you would need to get a much lower price to offset the added expense of getting the new loan and that it would tie up so much more of your investing capital.

2. Get a strong disclaimer from the sellers that says they understand you are taking title "subject to" the loan(s) and what that means. The CYS, or cover yourself, addendum we use states that the sellers *will not commit any action or make any statement orally or in writing that could cause the existing lender(s) to call the existing loan due.*

3. Make sure you live up to all your commitments to the sellers. One reason the sellers might call up their lender is if an unscrupulous investor didn't do what he or she promised.

4. Make sure you coach the sellers on what to do if the lender writes or calls them. You don't want a problem caused simply out of ignorance. Ask the sellers to forward all lender mail to you. In fact, have them sign a change of address letter to the lender asking the lender to send all correspondence about their loan to your address. If the lender calls, train the sellers to be "busy" and not talk with the lender until you have talked with the lender on the phone.

5. Owe the sellers money. Nothing keeps sellers living up to their promises like your having the leverage of owing them money. This is not to say you should overpay for the property just to owe the sellers money, but if you have to pay them money, see if you can make some of it payable down the road.

PITFALL #17: SELLER'S DISAPPEARING ONCE YOU'VE BOUGHT THE PROPERTY AND YOU NEED A SIGNATURE

The best way to cover yourself on this risk is to get the seller to sign a *limited power of attorney* that authorizes you to sign on the seller's behalf on all matters concerning this one specific property. (For more details, including a sample copy of a limited power of attorney form, see *Making Big Money Investing in Real Estate Without Tenants, Banks, or Rehab Projects*, pages 73–75.)

PITFALL #18: HAVING LIABILITY EVEN WHEN YOU ASSIGN YOUR CONTRACT

If you choose to flip your deal to another investor for a fast cash profit, make sure you get a signed release from both the buyer and the seller. Also, if your contract with the seller allowed you to buy the property "subject to" the existing financing, make sure you require that your assignee (the investor you're selling the deal to) signs a wraparound mortgage or an All-Inclusive Trust Deed to protect the seller. (You'll learn about these in Chapter 8.) Finally, be willing to step back in if the assignee ever defaults. (Ask your seller to save your contact information in case the assignee is more than 30 days late in making payments.) Not only is this the right thing to do, but it's also good business—you just might profit from the house twice!

PITFALL #19: SELLER'S CLAIMING DURESS

Whenever you're buying a property from a seller in foreclosure, you're buying from someone in a vulnerable position. While you will operate with integrity, be careful that a bitter seller who's mad at the world doesn't make claims stating you forced him or her into the deal. To protect yourself, always operate at arm's length in the deal. Don't demand that the seller deed the property to you on your first visit or refuse to allow the seller to have an advisor at the closing. Make sure you encourage the seller to make his or her decision independently and to invite a third-party advisor to any meetings if the seller wants that advisor there.

Also, include a clause such as the following in your purchase contract and ask the seller to initial it:

> *Seller hereby acknowledges that all negotiations and dealings with the Buyer have been and are at arm's length and that no duress or undue influence has been exerted by Buyer on Seller or any member of Seller's family in connection with this purchase and sale of this Property.*

PITFALL #20: SELLER'S CLAIMING MISREPRESENTATION

Because the sellers are under stress, you must protect yourself from their coming back later, claiming you tricked them into making the deal by misrepresenting certain things. The simplest way to protect yourself is to put everything you and the sellers agree on in writing. Also, follow up every important phone conversation with a letter explaining what both parties discussed and agreed to (see Pitfall #23 for more on this point). We recommend that you include in your final contract a "merger" clause stating this agreement is the full and final expression of exactly what you and the sellers did and did not agree to.

Here's the legalese version of a merger clause:

> *This agreement represents the full and final understanding between the parties. No agreements or representations, unless specifically incorporated into this agreement, shall be binding upon any of the parties.*

Here's another clause that we encourage you to put in your agreement with the seller:

Seller understands and is aware that the present fair market value of the Property is probably much higher than the purchase price set forth in this agreement. Seller hereby expressly waives any and all claims to potential or actual profit, income, or other sums in excess of the amount stated above in this agreement that comes from the Buyer's reselling the property or Buyer's rights under this agreement. Furthermore, Seller hereby acknowledges that the purchase price stated herein is fair and equitable and is in the Seller's best interests, and that the Seller's decision to sell was based on the Seller and that the Seller has not relied on any representation(s) of Buyer that is (are) not expressly contained in this agreement.

(For more information on how you can get all the contracts and agreements we use in our investing on CD-ROM, go to *www.ResultsNow.com.*)

PITFALL #21: SELLER'S BACKING OUT OF THE DEAL

If the sellers want out of the deal for valid reasons and within a reasonable period of time (up to three days after signing the deal), gracefully let them out of it. If, however, they want to back out of the deal because, two weeks later, they get a better offer from another investor, that's not fair to you. In this case, we recommend you hold them to the deal. In fact, we recommend that if the sellers ever want to back out of the deal after a few days and if you've spent significant money or time working on it, you make them pay you something to cancel the agreement. That's being fair to both of you.

To protect yourself from a seller's backing out, make sure you always record a Memorandum of Agreement (see Figure 6.1) against the property if you don't close within two days. A better way to close on the property quickly is by having the sellers deed you the house "subject to" existing financing. Insist that you still have the option of backing out of the deal if, after your due diligence, you discover something you don't like.

FIGURE 6.1 *Memorandum of Agreement*

RECORDING REQUESTED BY:

WHEN RECORDED MAIL AND
UNLESS OTHERWISE SHOWN BELOW,
MAIL TAX STATEMENTS TO:

SPACE ABOVE THIS LINE FOR RECORDER'S USE

Memorandum of Agreement

Be the world hereby apprised that I/we _____ (Obligor)
have entered into an agreement with _____ (Obligee)
wherein the Obligor has agreed to sell the below described property to the Obligee:
<<Property Legal>>.
Anyone dealing in and with the subject property should contact Obligee at:

_____

regarding the terms of this purchase agreement and the parties' respective rights thereunder.
IN WITNESS WHEREOF, the parties have signed this agreement.
Dated _____
STATE OF _____)
COUNTY OF _____) S.S.

On _____ before me, _____ ,
personally appeared _____ , personally known to me (or proved
to me on the basis of satisfactory evidence) to be the person(s) whose name(s) is/are subscribed to
the within instrument and acknowledged to me that he/she/they executed the same in his/her/their
authorized capacity(ies) and that by his/her/their signature(s) on the instrument the person(s), or the
entity upon behalf of which the person(s) acted, executed the instrument.

WITNESS my hand and official seal.

_____   _____
        Obligor   Date

_____   _____
        Obligor   Date

_____
            Signature

MAIL TAX STATEMENTS AS DIRECTED ABOVE
MY COMMISSION EXPIRES: _____

In the event you do back out of the deal, make sure you put down in writing that you can simply quitclaim the property back to the sellers and cancel the agreement with no further liability.

> ■ **Success Team—Commercial Coach Stephen's Story**
>
> I was buying a house from a highly motivated seller named Walter. I was so busy in the office that I delayed the closing for a week to complete another project. The day before the closing, I spent about three hours drawing up all the documents and getting ready for the closing to be held at my office at 10:00 AM the following day. The next day, the seller called me at 9:00 AM, only to tell me he'd found another solution to his problem. While I talked with the seller about how much he was willing to pay me to let him out of the agreement, all I kept thinking was that *this was my fault*. I never should have waited a week to close. I should have closed a few days after we signed the deal and made it clear we wouldn't make payments on the house for 30 days or so.
>
> The moral to the story is that when you have a motivated seller ready to deed the property over to you—let him or her do it immediately. And then, with your name on the title, conduct your due diligence before you invest any serious money in the deal. ■

PITFALL #22: INVESTING IN YOUR OWN NAME

In today's litigious world, you're taking your financial life in your own hands if you invest without at least one layer of liability protection in place. For the average investor, that means forming a limited liability company (LLC) and always operating from behind that protective screen. This is even more important if you are starting your investing business with significant assets you've already accumulated, such as a pension, a business you own, a personal residence with a lot of equity, or other rental properties you own. Invest the time not only in forming a limited liability company or corporation to protect yourself but in learning how to operate it so it's properly maintained. Hold annual meetings, with members' resolutions, and never commingle funds. (You'll find more information on the best ways to protect your assets in your Web Bonus Pack in Appendix A.)

■ **Success Team—Coach Robb's Story**

It's important to make sure you have the right entities set up, but remember that nothing happens until you take action. Some people don't take action until everything is completed and perfect, but everything will *never* be perfect. I've seen people wait until they get their business cards perfect, and their letterhead perfect, and their pencils sharpened to a fine point, and signs on their doors, and phone lines installed. The list goes on and on.

Make sure you remember and follow the most fundamental coaching advice I can give you—*act* on the ideas you've learned in this book.   ■

PITFALL #23: NOT PAPERING YOUR TRAIL

After a while, all deals look alike; the details, no matter how clear they were in the beginning, start to blur. Make sure you meticulously document each deal. This includes logging important conversations you hold with your sellers and your buyers or renters. Note the date and time you talked along with the important items you discussed. An easy way to do this without having it become a burden is to simply send an email stating, "Here's a quick summary of what we've agreed to." List what you've agreed to, then end up with a statement like, "If this is different from what you remember, please let me know; otherwise, I'll rely on what I've listed here as being accurate."

You can also send written letters if needed to clarify the main points you discussed and to establish a clear paper trail of what was agreed on. The secret here is to get the details down without getting obsessive about it.

■ Success Team—Peter's Story
I heard from one of our Mentorship students named Stacy about a training she took from someone outside The Mentor Family who insisted on writing down every word someone said while on the phone with him. Stacy said that he admitted to secretly recording conversations and then going back to transcribe them word for word. I told Stacy I felt sorry for someone who lived with a level of uncertainty that caused him to try to control relationships in this manner. I think that if someone believes everyone is trying to take advantage, then that belief will likely come true for that person. ■

PITFALL #24: TAKING PERSONAL RESPONSIBILITY FOR SELLER'S SITUATION

All investors must find the right balance between caring about the seller and taking on responsibility for the seller's situation. You can't help the seller by being a philanthropist. First and foremost, you're running a business. While you're committed to "win-win or no deal," this doesn't mean you can "save" every seller. In fact, you shouldn't try to save the seller at all.

We've watched many investors struggle trying to help a seller when the numbers just can't be made to work. Be careful of win-lose negotiating in which you sacrifice your need to make a profit to help a seller. In the end, this type of negotiating only makes things worse because you won't be able to live up to your side of the agreement.

■ Success Team—Coach Juli's Story

It was hard for me early on; I wanted to "save" every seller I met. I finally came to realize that while I could always empathize with them and hear them out, I wasn't willing to step over the line and take their situation on my back. That wouldn't be fair to me or my family. Plus, it would mean I couldn't help other sellers because I'd soon be out of business.

The place I settled into is one of listening respectfully and compassionately. I clearly let the seller know where I stand in the deal from the start. If I don't see a way to make a profit in the deal, I tell the sellers up front that it won't be a fit for me. Then I give them helpful suggestions about what to do. Not only does this help me keep my investing business in balance with my family and other commitments, but sellers appreciate the up-front manner with which I work with them.   ■

SUMMARY

So there are all 24 foreclosure pitfalls and how you can safely sidestep them. Use them as a guide to help you navigate the sometimes perilous world of foreclosure investing. As a quick summary, following is a list of the 24 pitfalls:

- Pitfall #1: Letting the sellers stay in the house
- Pitfall #2: Renting the property back to the sellers
- Pitfall #3: Putting *serious* money in the deal before the sellers vacate
- Pitfall #4: Giving sellers all their money *before* the final walk-through
- Pitfall #5: Putting serious money in the deal before completing due diligence
- Pitfall #6: Not accurately determining the real market value of the property

- Pitfall #7: Not checking the title carefully enough
- Pitfall #8: Not buying title insurance if you put serious money into the deal
- Pitfall #9: Not running a credit check on the sellers
- Pitfall #10: Seller's declaring a bankruptcy
- Pitfall #11: Buying only half a house
- Pitfall #12: Not getting the property professionally inspected
- Pitfall #13: Messing up your paperwork
- Pitfall #14: Not following your state's foreclosure laws
- Pitfall #15: Falling into the insurance trap
- Pitfall #16: Seller's pushing to get the loan called due
- Pitfall #17: Seller's disappearing once you've bought the property and you need a signature
- Pitfall #18: Having liability even when you assign your contract
- Pitfall #19: Seller's claiming duress
- Pitfall #20: Seller's claiming misrepresentation
- Pitfall #21: Seller's backing out of the deal
- Pitfall #22: Investing in your own name
- Pitfall #23: Not papering your trail
- Pitfall #24: Taking personal responsibility for situation of sellers

Use these pitfalls to help you navigate the perilous world of foreclosure investing. As part of your Bonus Web Pack in Appendix A, we've included a special report titled "Final Deal Checklist—The 27 Questions You Must Ask Before You Move Forward on Any Deal." This special report may be downloaded for free. It will help you take one last look at any deal and ensure it's smart to move forward.

In the next chapter, you'll learn how to turn your deals into quick cash profits. This is especially important if you want to use your foreclosure investing to generate immediate cash flow.

7

HOW TO FLIP YOUR DEALS FOR QUICK CASH PROFITS

Before we discuss how to turn your deals for quick cash profits, let's recap all the ways you can make money with any real estate deal.

SEVEN PROFIT CENTERS IN YOUR DEAL

Prior to exploring in detail the three steps involved in flipping or wholesaling your deals, we provide the following recap of the seven profit centers, or ways you can make money, in any real estate transaction:

1. *Cash flow.* This is simply the difference between the income the property generates and the expenses it costs.
2. *Amortization.* This fancy word means the equity pay-down of the underlying loan(s) on the property. Each time you pay the lender on most loans, a portion goes toward principal, and a chunk pays the interest. Over time, you pay the loan

down to zero and own the property free and clear. This is called the amortization of the loan.

3. *Tax benefits.* One of the last remaining tax breaks for the average person is real estate. You get to write off the interest paid, insurance, real estate taxes, and, best of all, depreciation.

4. *Appreciation.* Over time, most property goes up in value. And while this is usually a cyclical phenomenon, in just about every area of the country, this cycle keeps going higher and higher. In fact, the average rate of appreciation on a national average over the past 40 years was more than 6 percent. You can make a fortune when you combine this increase of value with your leveraging into a property using other people's money or other people's loans.

5. *Buying below value.* Because you'll be buying many of your foreclosures at bargain prices, another profit center will come from skillfully negotiating price.

6. *Discounting debt.* As discussed in Chapter 3, sometimes you can make extra money by getting lien holders or creditors to take less than they're owed as full payment, thus building more profit into the deal for yourself.

7. *Forfeited nonrefundable deposits and option payments.* When people you've sold a property to (or at least taken a non-refundable deposit from to hold the property) back out of the deal, you may make several thousand dollars extra by keeping their nonrefundable payment to you. (More on this in Chapter 8.)

Depending on which exit strategy you use with your property, you'll be able to tap into some or even all of the seven profit centers you've just learned about. In this chapter, you'll learn how to turn your deal for a fast cash profit. In the next chapter, you'll learn how to structure your properties for maximum long-term wealth accumulation.

You've already learned from Chapter 3 that you can sell deals you don't want to keep. This means either selling the contract for a cash *assignment fee* or selling the house quickly to a retail buyer. Let's get into the three specific steps needed to make this happen.

STEP ONE: LOCK UP THE PROPERTY UNDER CONTRACT

Before you can ever flip a deal, you need to sign an agreement to buy that property from the seller. By applying all the marketing and negotiating strategies you've already learned, you'll find many deals to put under contract. Some you'll hang on to for the long term; others you'll sell for a quick profit.

You'll be signing up and selling two types of deals to other investors—cash deals or terms deals. With *cash deals*, you'll negotiate a discounted cash price, typically 60 percent to 70 percent of the "as is" value, in exchange for the seller's getting all the cash at the closing. For example, imagine you met sellers who own a $300,000 house that needs $20,000 for repairs. The sellers can't make their monthly payment, let alone fix up their house. So you negotiate a sale price of $190,000 cash with the sellers. You're thrilled because your price is 68 percent of the "as is" value. (The "as is" value is the after-repair value [ARV] of the property minus the cost of the work that needs to be done on the house to make it salable at that ARV.)

But you don't want to do the rehab or find the $190,000. Instead, you simply sell the deal to another investor who specializes in rehabs in your area. This new investor pays you $15,000 cash for you to assign your contract to him or her. Then he or she moves forward and buys the house from the seller. Once you have assigned your contract to the new investor and collected your $15,000 check, that's it. The investor you sold the deal to will do the rehab project and net $50,000 or more when reselling the property to a retail buyer (see Figure 7.1). Everyone wins.

FIGURE 7.1 *Sample Numbers of Wholesaling Cash Deal*

Step One: You Sign Up the Deal

After-repair value (ARV)	$300,000
"As is" value (ARV less repair costs)	$280,000
Your price	$190,000

Step Two: You Assign Your Contract to Another Investor

Your contract price	$190,000
Assignment fee you collect	$15,000
New investor's price	$205,000
Your net profit	$15,000

Step Three: You're Done . . . New Investor Rehabs, Then Resells the Property

ARV	$300,000
New investor's price	($205,000)
Repair cost	($20,000)
Closing costs	($3,000)
Holding costs	($4,000)
Commission when selling	($18,000)
New investor's net profit	$50,000

A *terms deal* is a deal in which either the seller agrees to wait for a period of time to get some or all of his or her equity or in which little money goes to the seller. For example, imagine that same seller in the previous example owes $240,000 against the property. This time, you negotiate to buy the property for $245,000 by paying the seller $5,000 cash and taking title "subject to" the seller's existing $240,000 loan. And this time, you have a contract to purchase that house for 88 percent of the "as is" value, but you have great financing in place because you are buying "subject to" the seller's loan. Again, you decide that you don't want to hang on to this deal but want to turn it for a fast profit. So you find a local investor willing to pay $10,000 to buy this deal from you. You make a fast $10,000, and your investor gets a deal that requires only $15,000 down and has long-term financing in place in the form of the seller's existing loan. Again, everyone wins.

Whether you sign up a cash deal or a terms deal, typically you can flip both types and turn a cash profit in 30 to 60 days. Here are the formulas to guide you as you determine how much to sell your deal for. With a cash deal, look to lock up the property for as low a price as possible, but make sure you're agreeing to pay *no more* than 65 percent to 70 percent of the "as is" value. Typically, you'll be able to find an investor to buy the property for between 70 percent and 80 percent of the "as is" value. This leaves you with a profit of between 5 percent and 15 percent of that value. Not bad for someone who never has to swing a hammer or raise a paintbrush.

A student of ours from Dayton, Ohio, got a call from a motivated seller who was responding to a flyer she put out on all the houses in her farm area. The seller was elderly and in poor health and just couldn't take care of the property anymore. She was four months behind on her payments. Our student put the property under contract, then flipped the deal to another local investor for $4,500 profit.

When formulating how much to sell a terms deal for, first calculate what you think the conservative net profit will be for this new investor. Then charge 10 percent to 20 percent of that long-term profit as your price to sell the deal.

Jerry, a retired General Motors employee in Michigan, did a mailing to expired listings (people who had listed their homes with a real estate agent but their property had not sold during the listing period). He found an owner who had inherited a house from his mother. Jerry agreed to buy the property for $20,000 with $2,000 cash to the seller, $1,900 of back payments, and "subject to" the seller's existing first mortgage. Then he sold the deal to another buyer and made $10,000 from it.

Here's another example of how easy this can be. We received an email from Doug, an investor who lives in California. Doug found a motivated seller of a two-bedroom condo in Santa Barbara who needed to unload this property quickly. Initially, the seller said no to Doug's offer to buy the unit "subject to" the existing financing. But one month later, he came back to Doug to take the deal. So Doug called a friend who lived in Chicago who had told Doug he wanted to move to that area. His friend sent him a $6,000 cashier's check the next day to buy out Doug's contract.

The Secret Clause That Allows You to Flip Your Deal

While any contract that doesn't specifically say it is "nonassignable" is legally assignable, you should make sure your purchase contract specifically says it is assignable. Simply sign up the deal with your name, or better yet your company's or LLC's name, "or assigns," as the Buyer. You can do this easily by preprinting the "or assigns" into your purchase contract (see Figure 7.2) so you never forget to include it.

FIGURE 7.2 *Excerpt from Purchase Agreement with "Or Assigns" Preprinted into the Agreement*

> John and Sally Homeowners, as Seller, and Home Buyers, LLC *or assigns* as Buyer, hereby agree that the Seller shall sell and the Buyer shall buy the following described property UPON THE TERMS AND CONDITIONS HEREINAFTER SET FORTH, which shall include the STANDARDS FOR REAL ESTATE TRANSACTIONS set forth within this agreement.

If You're Still Wondering How You Can Sell a House You Don't Own . . .

If you like the idea of making a quick cash profit but are still struggling with how you can sell a house you don't own to another investor, you are not alone. Many of our students have struggled with that idea when they first got started. The key distinction is that you are *not* selling the house; you are selling your *rights* under a contract to buy that house at a set price and terms.

This happens all the time in the real estate world. For example, a bank often sells a loan it originated to another party. It gets paid a fee to assign its rights under a promissory note and deed or trust/mortgage to this other party. Or a tenant subleases a property to a subtenant. These are examples of selling a contractual right—in one case to receive payments from a loan and in the other to rent out the use of a property to a third party for a fee. Again, as long as no language in a contract makes it nonassignable, all contracts are assignable.

The best part of assigning your interests in a contract to another party is that you don't need to be a licensed real estate agent to do this. You are *not* representing a seller or helping people sell their house. You are acting as a principal, locking up a contract, and selling your interest in that contract for a profit. You don't need any kind of license to do this.

Take the case of Gary, a student who lives in San Diego. Gary called an old friend one day and found out his friend was in trouble with a house he owned in Phoenix. Gary's friend owed $145,562 on a house worth only $130,000. So Gary got the second mortgage holder to accept a short sale of less than three cents on the dollar. He then turned and quickly sold the property to a retail cash buyer for $123,000. All totaled, Gary split the $26,000 profit he made 50-50 with his old friend. As you can imagine, both of them were thrilled.

STEP TWO: FIND A BUYER FOR YOUR DEAL

You have the following three sources of potential buyers for your deal:

1. Retail buyers
2. Other investors
3. In-house "buyers list"

A retail buyer is the average home buyer who is looking to buy a house. *Retail* buyers might buy the house if you give them a good price. For example, you get a call from a seller responding to one of your postcards. This seller is two months away from losing his or her house to foreclosure. The house is worth about $250,000 in its current condition, and with about $5,000 worth of cosmetic work, it would sell for $275,000.

You meet with the seller and agree on a cash price of $180,000 with the closing date in 28 days. You find a buyer who'd like to own the house and is willing to pay as much as $220,000 to take the house in "as is" condition. Your buyer gets a house for $30,000 below its real market value, and you make $40,000 (less your marketing costs and any share of closing costs you agree to pay). (See Figure 7.3.)

We'll go into more detail about how to handle this closing when we walk you through the final step of wholesaling a deal. For the moment, it's important to understand that selling the deal to a retail buyer will always make you more money than selling it to another investor. That makes sense because, in essence, you're cutting out the second middleman of the new investor. That's why you prefer to sell your deal to a retail buyer.

The second source of potential buyers is other investors. You want to find someone interested in paying you a cash assignment fee for the deal. In our current example, imagine you tried to find a retail buyer but weren't able to. But you did get an investor who

FIGURE 7.3 *Selling to a Retail Buyer versus Another Investor*

ARV	$275,000
"As is" value	$250,000
Your price	$180,000

Option One: Your Preferred Choice—Sell to a Retail Buyer

Pays you	$220,000
Your price	($180,000)
Your costs	
Closing	($2,000)
Marketing	($1,000)
Your net profit	**$37,000**

Option Two: Your Second Choice—Sell to Another Investor

You collect $10,000 assignment fee

Your investor goes on to rehab and resell property

ARV	$275,000
New investor's price	($190,000)
Repairs	($5,000)
Closing costs (twice)	($4,000)
Holding costs	($5,000)
Real estate commission (selling)	($16,500)
New investor's net profit	**$54,500**

was willing to pay $10,000 for the deal. You decide that $10,000 for the five hours' work you have tied into the deal is a decent hourly wage so you take it. (Later in this chapter, you'll learn how to find these investors—again, see Figure 7.3.)

The third source of buyers for your deal is the in-house "buyers list" you've been cultivating. As both retail buyers and other investors call you about deals you have for sale, doesn't it make sense that if you don't have something they want at the moment, you add them to your buyers list? Of course. Yet many investors forget to build these two important lists as they meet new prospective buyers. (Later in this chapter, we'll discuss the best ways to cultivate and use these two lists.)

The Biggest Secret to Flipping a Deal Fast

Most investors spend a few weeks looking for a retail buyer. If that doesn't work, then they contact their in-house investors list. If they still can't find a buyer, they get desperate and start advertising for other investors to buy the deal. Usually, these investors run out of time. Remember, the really good deals usually have a tight time crunch to make them work.

In our opinion, the real secret to flipping a deal fast is to look for all three types of buyers at the same time. Then you take the first decent offer to put *cash* in your hand. Simple as that.

Here's how this works in the real world. First, put your For Sale sign out in the front yard. Because it's hard to raise the price once your buyer sees it, this sign should advertise the property for sale to retail buyers. Investors won't mind that you're giving them a lower price. You can get this sign made for $30 to $60 at a local sign shop.

Also, flood the area with 30 to 40 handmade For Sale signs. These signs should be written with a fat black marker on sheets of poster board you've cut in half. After all, if you were looking for a bargain, would you rather see a fancy professional sign or a desperate handmade sign? Your buyers prefer the handmade

FIGURE 7.4 *Sample Neighborhood Signs to Market Your Deal*

> Foreclosure!
> 3 Bed / 2 Bath
> 888-555-4567
> 24-hr. Rec. Msg.

signs, too. They can almost smell the bargain they're going to get. (See Figure 7.4.) In fact, you'll probably get more investors calling from your signs than retail buyers.

You'll notice that we sent all our callers to our "24-hour recorded message." You'll likely get flooded with calls. Let technology help you screen them out by setting up voice mail to take these calls. (See *Making Big Money Investing in Real Estate Without Tenants, Banks, or Rehab Projects*, pages 192–94, for detailed instructions on using a recorded message when marketing your properties.)

Three Little-Known Power Ad Secrets

In addition to using signs to market your property, tap into the power of classified ads to get your phone ringing nonstop. Here are three little-known secrets to pumping up the response from all your classified advertising.

Secret 1: Use an attention-grabbing headline on your ad. The first three to seven words need to be a headline that grabs the attention of prospective buyers and locks their eyes onto your ad. If you want to find a buyer fast, use any of the following possible attention grabbers:

- Desperate Seller!
- Foreclosure!
- Forced Sale!
- Stranded Seller Must Sell in 7 Days or Less!
- Personal Circumstances Force Fast Sale!

Secret 2: Use attractive terms to sell your house fast. You'll learn more about selling with owner financing in the next chapter, but for the moment, read through the following list of words that will attract a buyer's attention:

- Take over payments on my loan!
- Owner financing!
- No bank qualifying!
- 100% owner financing!
- Rent to own!

Secret 3: Use a low price to generate tons of calls. Your goal is to create an atmosphere of competition to bid up the price on the house. Be careful not to make an offer to prospective buyers that will force you to sell too cheaply.

Figure 7.5 shows several sample ads you can use to advertise your properties. Notice that some are directed at investors, while others are for retail buyers.

FIGURE 7.5 *Sample Power Ads to Flip a Deal Fast*

> Foreclosure Pending. Need quick sale! 3 Bed/2 Bath. Will discount 10%–15% below market if you can close fast. 619-555-4567 24-hr. msg.

> Desperate, MUST SELL! 3 Bed/2 Bath House. Personal Circumstances Force Fast Sale. 877-555-4567 x 34. 24-hr. rec. msg.

> Desperate Seller must sell in 14 days or lose house. Worth $311,850, will seriously consider any offer over $279,500 if you can close fast.

Building Your In-House Buyers List

As buyers respond to your marketing campaigns, make sure always to capture and save their contact information on your in-house buyers list. Your goal is to build two lists that will allow you to turn your flipper deals faster and for more money than you ever could by advertising for brand-new buyers each time you whole-sale a deal.

The first list is your retail buyers list, which includes all those people who have contacted you about buying one of your homes to live in themselves.

■ Success Team—Robb's Story

I don't use any fancy software program to track my buyers list. I simply keep all their contact information in a spreadsheet on my computer. Besides their names, phone numbers, and email addresses, I also capture what type of home they are looking for and in what area. In addition, I capture the amount of down payment they have to work with, how much of a house they can qualify for a loan on, and how high a monthly payment they can afford to pay. When I want to sell a house fast, I first go through my buyers list, send out a quick email to everyone, and call up those qualified for this specific house. ■

The second list is your investors list, which includes all the other investors you have met or who have called you about a prior deal you flipped. Again, keep track of their contact information, especially email addresses. We love using email to market a property to our investors list because it's fast, effective, and *free*!

To build your list, go to your local real estate investors association monthly meetings. (For a state-by-state list of what groups are active, contact the American Real Estate Investors Association website at *www.americanreia.com.*) At your local association meeting, you'll be able to network with dozens of other investors who are looking for deals.

Also, get an email address for every investor you can find and send an email message such as the one in Figure 7.6. This is your way of building your list of prospective investors. Beginning investors tend to forget to get the email address of every investor who calls about a deal. Don't lose out on the chance of building your investors list; it's the fastest way to turn a deal for a quick cash profit.

FIGURE 7.6   *Sample Email to Send to Prospective Investors to Survey Them*

Subject: Investor Special

Hi there,

    Thanks for emailing me about the investor special. This one is not available but I have been finding more properties lately than I am able to deal with due to my limited time.

    I'll do my best to email the details of any deals that I come across so that you can be one of the first to get a look at them. Because I negotiate my profits on the way into my deals, most properties I'll let you know about are 15 percent to 25 percent below market, and some even come with creative financing in place.

    If you can take a moment to answer the questions below, this will help me to determine what types of deal you are looking for. Occasionally, I'll find an absolute steal that needs some money to get the home quickly before anyone else gets it.

How much cash could you have at closing within 10 days (if you knew it was a great deal)? $ _____

Which of the following exit strategies have you used or are you comfortable with?
____ Fix and resell to retail buyer
____ Sell on rent-to-own to tenant-buyer
____ Hold as long-term rental
____ Sell with nonqualifying financing to nonconforming buyers

How many deals have you done? _____

How do you calculate a "good deal"? (Please be specific; e.g., percent of after-repair value, or you must make at least $10,000, etc.) _____

Lowest-price homes you'd consider: $ _____
Highest-price homes you'd consider: $ _____
Preferred AFTER-REPAIR price range: $ _____
Areas you prefer to invest in: _____
Areas you will NOT invest in: _____
Which types of repair work are you comfortable with? _____

Your Name: _____
Address: _____
Best Day Phone: _____
Other Phone # to try: _____
Fax: _____
Email: _____

If you prefer, you can print this form and fax it to me at 303-555-1234 or just hit reply and put your answers in the appropriate places.

Thanks,
Brenda Investor
303-555-1256

    P.S. I know that I asked a lot of questions. It's just that I want to know exactly what deals I should send your way to save you time. By taking five minutes now to share your criteria for a deal that makes you money, you will save hours in looking for new deals. You can leverage your time by letting me be one of your bird dogs spotting potential deals for you. I make an assignment fee, you go on to even bigger profits, and everyone wins!

    P.P.S. From time to time, I'll be sending you emails that list new potential deals for you to consider. These emails will say "Bargain Finder Report" in the subject line. Have a great day!

■ Success Team—Commercial Coach Stephen's Story

Flipping foreclosure deals to other investors is my preferred method of creating monthly cash flow. As soon as I was comfortable doing flips on my own, I decided to jump into Level Two. I now have two people who work for me as buyers in my office. They qualify and meet with homeowners willing to sell for 50 percent to 60 percent of value in exchange for a quick cash sale.

Make sure you build systems like this as you grow! I have developed a list of other investors who love to rehab properties and are always on the lookout for new deals. The three steps are: get it under contract, email details to your investors list, and collect $10,000 to $20,000 as your assignment fee.   ■

STEP THREE: CLOSE WITH YOUR BUYER

Once you find a buyer who wants to buy your deal, you'll need to set up a closing with this person. A *closing* is a fancy name for a time to sit down and sign all the final paperwork that assigns your interest in the deal to this new buyer and for you to collect your check from your new buyer.

If you're flipping the deal to another investor, this closing is fast and easy. Simply get this investor to bring you a cashier's check for the amount of your assignment fee. Collect this check first, then sign an Assignment of Real Estate Contract form (see Figure 7.7). Give this buyer all your original contract paperwork with the seller, and you've completed the deal.

■ Success Team—Cheryl's Story

I believe it's important that I make sure the person I sell a deal to can perform with the seller. While I'm *technically* done with the deal once I assign it over to my buyer, I still stay in contact with the seller to make sure he or she gets treated right by this new buyer. I know I don't have to do this; it's simply the right way to do business.   ■

FIGURE 7.7 *Sample Assignment of Real Estate Contract Form*

Assignment of Real Estate Contract

FOR VALUE RECEIVED, the undersigned wholesaler (Assignor) hereby assigns, transfers, and sets over to _____ (Assignee) all rights, title, and interest held by the Assignor in and to the following described contract:

The Assignee hereby assumes and agrees to perform all the remaining and executory obligations of the Assignor under the Contract in good faith and within the time periods established by said Contract. Assignee agrees to indemnify and hold the Assignor harmless from any claim or demand resulting from nonperformance by the Assignee. The Assignee hereby commits $_____ in certified funds as a nonrefundable deposit and will pay an additional compensation in the amount of $_____ prior to closing on the Contract. In the event that Assignee defaults on the Contract, then the nonrefundable deposit mentioned herein shall be retained as complete liquidated damages by Assignor and all rights to the above Contract will revert back to Assignor.

The Assignee agrees to defend, indemnify, and hold Assignor harmless for any deficiency or defect in the legality or enforceability of the terms of said Contract.

The Assignee agrees and understands that the Assignor is not acting as a real estate agent or broker, but rather the Assignor is a principal in the transaction who is selling their interest in the above-referenced Contract to Assignee.

This assignment shall be binding upon and inure to the benefit of the parties, their successors, and assigns.

This agreement is "subject to" the following conditions:

_____

_____

_____

Date of this agreement: _____

_____   _____
Wholesaler / Assignor   Assignee

If you're selling your deal to a retail buyer, you sometimes have to do more work to make the closing happen. If you are selling a terms deal in which your new buyer wants to buy the property to live in because of the easy financing in place, then this closing with your buyer is easy. For example, take our $250,000 house that needs $5,000 in repairs to be worth $275,000. You agreed with the seller to buy the property for $5,000 down and take over "subject to" the seller's $240,000 mortgage.

In this example, your retail buyer agrees to pay you $265,000 for the house in "as is" condition because you're letting the buyer get in with the existing financing in place. Your new buyer agrees to give you $25,000 cash, of which you give $5,000 to the seller and keep the other $20,000 as your profit. Your new buyer now gets title to the house and agrees to take over the monthly payments. (You'll learn more about this type of deal in Chapter 8.)

You could also have had your new buyer give you $20,000 and then assign him or her your contract with the seller. This would also work. (We'll go into the details of why we prefer the first way over assigning the deal to the new buyer in the next chapter.)

Why is flipping a cash deal to a retail buyer more work? Usually, the retail buyer will use a conventional loan to fund part or all of the purchase of the property. Whenever a conventional lender is involved, things become more complicated simply because this lender has all its own rules and requirements for doing things. But it's worth the extra effort—you'll make more money when you sell a deal to a retail buyer rather than to an investor.

Besides just getting a cash fee to assign your contract to a buyer, there are two more ways to accomplish your flip to a retail buyer when a conventional lender is involved. We aren't complicating this to impress you. It's just that when we started flipping deals in the various states we buy properties in, we soon learned that the textbook way of closing these deals didn't always work when conventional lenders were added to the equation. So you're about to learn the lessons of years of trial and error to find the winning formulas.

Imagine you have a house worth $325,000 in "as is" condition. The sellers are five weeks away from losing the property to the foreclosure auction. They owe $210,000 against the property and are $20,000 behind in payments. The house needs about $15,000 worth of cosmetic repairs to show well and be able to sell for its ARV of $375,000. Because you didn't want to do the rehab work, you negotiated the best cash price you could with the sellers, knowing you would flip the deal to someone else. After using all the negotiating ideas learned from this book (plus a few others you've picked up over the years), you got the sellers to agree on a price of $275,000.

You turn around and find a couple who want to buy the house in its "as is" condition for $315,000. They figure they're getting a great deal, and they're actually looking forward to fixing it up the way they want before they move in. And you're thrilled because you'll make $40,000 on this deal.

Now let's look at the two ways you can close this deal and get paid your $40,000. First, you can do a *simultaneous closing.* This means you close on the deal with your buyers and sellers at the same time, using your buyers' money to pay the sellers their $275,000, of which $230,000 goes to pay off the first mortgage and $45,000 goes to the sellers less their share of the closing costs. Your title or escrow company (whoever is doing the closing for you) sets up a double closing. You and the sellers meet in one conference room and sign all the documents needed to complete the transaction with the sellers. Then you walk down the hall into the separate closing room with your buyers and collect their money and deed the house over to them. Then the escrow agent takes the money the buyers' lender paid to pay off the existing lender, to pay the sellers their money, and to give you your $40,000 check. This is the easiest way to do the closing whenever you can. The key is that the buyers' lender will have to be open to funding the deal that involves a double closing. This works 30 percent to 50 percent of the time, depending on where you live.

The second way to handle the closing is a fallback if the lender won't let you do a simultaneous closing. You can take this three-party transaction—you, the sellers, and your buyers—and turn it into a two-party transaction. Because the buyers are the ones with all the money, you can't get rid of them. But you can temporarily get rid of the sellers by having them deed you the property "subject to" the existing loan. Now that you are on the title, the buyers' lender will be satisfied, and you can close directly with your new buyers. You simply agree on paper with your sellers that the escrow instructions will order the escrow agent to use the new buyers' funds to pay off the existing loan, to then give the sellers their share of the proceeds, and finally to give what's left to you, the investor.

Again, we know this looks like a hassle, and it is. But in the real world of investing, sometimes the textbook moves like simultaneous closings don't work and you need a street-smart backup. That's why we shared this fallback strategy with you to get the deal to close.

 ■ **Success Team—Robb's Story**

It can sometimes be a total hassle to deal with a buyer's lender to make a deal work. When you are putting in the effort to get your deal done, make sure to measure results the same we do with our Mentorship students. While it's great to talk about success, we won't give up until we are able to take two deals with each student all the way to the bank together. "Taking It to the Bank" means that for your effort, you don't just dream about it or have it as a "maybe someday," but that you actually get to collect a fat check and take it to the bank. Keep saying it over and over to yourself—I'm Taking It to the Bank . . . I'm Taking It to the Bank. ■

 ■ **Success Team—Commercial Coach Rob's Story**

Be careful that you don't get caught on the treadmill of flipping deals. Yes, you can make some exciting money by flipping properties, but when you stop working, your income stops flowing. If you need quick cash, then flip deals to create that cash flow. But also develop the resources to build a portfolio of properties for your long-term financial freedom. I look at flipping deals as a way to make money from deals that I wouldn't want to have to do all the rehab work on or deal with over time.

You can ignore this advice if you want and flip all the deals you sign up. You'll make lots of money. I just want you to have more than money. I want you to have the freedom to be wealthy and the security to enjoy your future without having to race around hunting up your next deal. This means passive, *residual* income, and this means building a portfolio of investment properties to hold over time. Using Peter's and The Mentor Family's advice, I've moved from working for a corporation and traveling non-stop to being able to work from home, starting with single-family houses. Now most of my investments are in big commercial deals that give me passive income and quite big chunks of profit. This has allowed me finally to be with my wife and kids. The lesson is to make sure that you are looking ahead so you can plan several steps in advance of where you are at the moment.   ■

8

INVESTING FOR LONG-TERM WEALTH BUILDUP

One of the decisions you will have to make in your investing business is whether you are going to invest for short-term cash flow or long-term wealth buildup or some hybrid of the two.

You have already learned how to turn your foreclosure deal into fast cash, so it's time to turn our attention to ways of structuring your properties for long-term equity buildup. Both are important. You need cash flow to have spendable income to support your family, but you need long-term equity growth to build the lifestyle and future you want for yourself.

> ■ **Success Team—Peter's Story**
>
> At our workshops, one of the most common questions is, "What do I wish I would have known when I got started investing that would have had the most dramatic positive impact on my success?" It's a great question that cuts straight past all the hype to the core

of what's essential. Here is my answer: I wish I had held on to more of the properties I bought. I look at the houses I turned in the early days of my investing after owning or controlling them for 12 months or less, and I think, *If only I still had those properties . . .*

In my first two years alone, if I still owned or controlled all the houses I had under contract, I would be about $3 million wealthier! And this is a very conservative estimate.   ■

The exit strategies you choose must meet the needs of your own situation. You may need to turn a quick cash profit like you need your next breath of air. Fair enough. If that's the case, use the ideas in Chapter 7 to turn your properties for fast cash. Just make sure to hold on to some of the properties you're buying for your future well-being. You don't want to get trapped in the rat race, always looking for the next deal to flip, and the next, and the next.

You may already have solid income, whether from a business, a job, or other investments. Great. In that case, you'll want to rely on the exit strategies described in this chapter to maximize your long-term wealth buildup. The best part of investing in fore-closures is that you control how much you make and when you make it.

STRATEGY 1: RENT OUT THE PROPERTY

While this book isn't about being a landlord, you should understand that this traditional way of holding on to properties over time has worked for thousands of investors. It's not our pre-ferred niche of investing, but we still use it as an exit strategy for a portion of our real estate portfolio. Just be aware that being a landlord can be a drag at times.

■ Success Team—Commercial Coach Rob's Story

I still have about 30 traditional rentals going. They provide good cash flow and allow me to hang on to the properties over the long haul. The biggest downside is that traditional rentals are time intensive. In the past, I handled this by forming my own property management company. But this still took so much energy away from my family and other investing activities. That's what led me to search out a better way to handle my growing portfolio. Today, the majority of my single-family home portfolio is structured on a rent-to-own basis.   ■

STRATEGY 2: SELL PROPERTIES ON A RENT-TO-OWN BASIS

One of our favorite exit strategies is to sell a property on a rent-to-own basis. Because you're putting someone with an owner's mentality (as opposed to a renter's mind-set) into the home, your property will likely be better cared for. And because you'll collect a hefty, nonrefundable option fee up front that's 3 percent to 5 percent of the value of the property, you're in a strong position to collect your rent each month from your tenant-buyer.

■ Success Team—Coach Robb's Story

I've noticed that when I use the rent-to-own exit strategy, I'm dealing with people who think of themselves as "homeowners" rather than as "renters." In my opinion, this makes offering your property on a rent-to-own basis a great holding strategy and turns your properties into hands-off rentals. I recommend pushing most or all of the day-to-day maintenance onto your tenant-buyer's shoulders. This, more than anything else, has helped me escape the landlord trap of tenants and toilets. Today, I spend less time managing my entire real estate portfolio than I did when I had several rental properties, which I converted to rent-to-own homes several years ago.   ■

For complete details on how to price, advertise, and sell properties successfully on a rent-to-own basis, see *Making Big Money Investing in Real Estate Without Tenants, Banks, or Rehab Projects* (pages 181–229).

STRATEGY 3: SELL WITH OWNER FINANCING

Considering that in many areas of the country, 75 percent or more of renters cannot qualify to purchase the median-priced house in that area with conventional financing, you probably don't need any convincing about nonbank financing's appeal to a huge percentage of would-be homebuyers.

Many potential buyers have credit problems or not enough income to qualify for traditional financing, so you'll find that when you offer one of your properties with owner financing, you'll get swamped with people who want to buy.

Owner financing simply means that you, the seller of a property, act as the bank. You finance the sale so your buyer doesn't have to go to a conventional lender and qualify for a traditional loan.

Most beginning investors see owner financing as an option only for properties they own free and clear. For example, suppose you have a house you own free and clear worth $400,000. You sell it to a buyer for a down payment of $40,000 (10 percent) and carry back the other $360,000 as a mortgage to be paid to you over the next five years. This is the best-known form of owner financing, where sellers act like the bank on a property they own free and clear. But as a savvy investor, you can tap into the power of owner financing in many more powerful ways.

■ Success Team—Coach Juli's Story

Remember talking about buying properties "subject to" the existing financing? You might not have realized it, but that's a form of owner financing. For example, say you find a seller of a $275,000 house who is four months behind in making payments. You agree to buy that house by making up the seller's back payments and taking title "subject to" the existing $245,000 loan. The sale solves the seller's problem, which is the looming foreclosure, and you get a house for about $6,500 in back payments with about $20,000 to $25,000 of equity. In essence, this is an owner-financed deal because you use the seller's existing loan as a way of leveraging yourself into the property.   ■

You can use this same concept when you sell a property by selling it "subject to" the existing financing. Continuing on with the previous example, you now have the house under contract, but you don't have the $8,000 you need to catch up the back payments and pay for closing costs. So you decide to sell the house with owner financing and let your new buyer give you the funds needed to bring the payments current. You advertise using techniques described later in this chapter, find a buyer who agrees to purchase the house for $290,000 with 10 percent down, and you carry back the balance. So now you collect $29,000 as a down payment, then use $8,000 to make up the back payments and pay for closing costs. You've just made $21,000 cash up front, plus you'll make another $8,000 on the back end (see Figure 8.1). And there are two more hidden profit centers we haven't shared with you yet.

FIGURE 8.1 *Sample Owner-Carry Deal*

Value	$275,000
Your price	$253,000
Existing first mortgage you took title "subject to"	$245,000
Your CASH costs up front	
Back payments	$6,500
Closing costs	$1,500
Your selling price	$290,000
Your purchase price	($253,000)
Your profit	$37,000
Form of your profits	
Cash	
Buyer's down payment	$29,000
Cash YOU put into deal	($8,000)
Net cash up front	$21,000
Note you carry for your buyer	$8,000

(Note: You'll also earn interest from the note you carry back for your buyer.)

■ Success Team—Coach Cheryl's Story

Look at your local Sunday paper. In many cities, more than 200 properties are offered for sale at any given time. Yet out of these 200, fewer than 20 will be offered with no bank financing. That means you're offering something that's scarce. Combine this with the fact that the average renter can't qualify to buy the median-priced home in most cities, and you recognize that not only is the *supply* limited but the *demand* is greater for an owner-financed house than for a traditionally financed one. I may not know much about economics, but even I know that when supply is limited and demand increases, prices must go up.

When I sell with owner financing, I typically get 5 percent to 10 percent above market value for the property—and without any real estate commission—simply because the financing has made the house more valuable! After all, your buyers are not really buying the house; they're buying the financing. Now, I don't get all this money up front, but I like creating a hands-off income stream that has a future payoff.   ■

Six Benefits to the Buyer for Using Owner Financing

Following are the six benefits you, the buyer, may experience when using owner financing:

1. *Fast closing.* You can close in as few as 72 hours. Just try that with a conventional lender!
2. *Easy monthly payments.* You're in control of structuring the payments. If you want, you can even charge interest-only payments, lowering the monthly payment.
3. *No banks to deal with.* This means no bureaucracy and red tape and loan committees to work through.
4. *Almost no paperwork to fill out.* Yes, you'll get a loan application from your buyers, but they'll save hours not having to fill out redundant bank forms and creating fancy loan application packets.
5. *Doesn't matter what their credit or income is like.* Depending on the amount of down payment buyers have to work with and the amount they can afford to pay you each month, you can work with buyers no matter what their credit is like.
6. *Flexible terms on the financing.* You can structure the financing to meet your buyer's needs. If your buyer needs two years to clean up his or her credit and then refinance, you can

set up the financing to have a balloon note due for the out-standing balance after two or three years. *You* are the one in control of structuring the financing.

Selling with owner financing is not the right fit for every situation, but it's a useful tool to have in your toolbox. Following are three reasons that might make selling one of your properties with owner financing the right exit strategy for you:

1. *You need a large amount of money up front.* Typically, you'll be able to collect 10 percent to 15 percent as a down payment. This can often be your source of funding to get into the deal. Or if you need money up front to live on, owner financing allows you to satisfy your immediate cash needs while still creating a passive income stream and back-end profit.

■ Success Team—Peter's Story

We bought a house in southern California with two of our Mentorship students, Mark and Trish. We bought the house "subject to" the existing financing. When we were planning our exit strategy, Mark and Trish said they wanted to get as much money up front from the sale as possible. We decided to sell the house with owner financing and got $25,000 of our total $28,000 profit up front within 60 days. ■

2. *You need to get a higher-than-market rent payment.* Because your buyer will get to write off the interest paid on the property, you can charge a significantly higher-than-market monthly rent payment and still save your buyer money over conventional financing.

■ Success Team—Coach Cheryl's Story

I was helping one of our Mentorship students structure a deal in Ohio. She had purchased a property from a seller who was in preforeclosure, but the monthly payment was $200 over the market rent for the house. I explained that by selling with owner financing, she could find a buyer willing to pay that much, which in this case was $1,100 a month. She did, in fact, find a buyer who paid her the $1,100 by selling the property on an installment land contract—a form of owner financing.   ■

3. *You want to make sure you will have no more responsibility with the property.* Even selling on a rent-to-own basis can require some property management on your part. By selling with owner financing, you truly do step into the hands-off role of passive institutional investor. Your buyer is legally responsible for everything involving the property, including making a payment to you each month. Also, because you're getting three to four times the up-front money than if you were selling on a rent-to-own basis, you can be much more secure knowing your buyer will take care of the property and live up to his or her side of the deal, including paying the monthly payments on time.

Take care that when you choose to sell a property with owner financing, you take steps to protect yourself. You'll learn about wraparound mortgages and land contracts soon, both of which are used to protect yourself when you are selling with owner financing. One of the best protections is having definite criteria for when you should *not* sell with owner financing.

Following are the three criteria for when you should *not* sell with owner financing:

1. *When your buyer doesn't have at least 10 percent to pay as a down payment.* If the buyer has less than this amount, don't sell the property with owner financing. You can sell it instead on a rent-to-own basis and agree that if the buyer pays you at least 10 percent down by a specific date, you will grant the option of having you carry back the financing. You should not give someone title to your property, be it legal title or equitable title, who hasn't paid you at least 10 percent down.

2. *When your buyer wants to buy with none of his or her own money.* While we love buying without any of our own money, rarely will we allow anyone to buy a property from us where we agree to help finance this new buyer but none of the buyer's own money is at stake. Why? We know, just as lenders know, that when a buyer has his or her own money at risk, the buyer is much more likely to live up to the terms and conditions of the loan.

3. *When you aren't getting enough profit in the deal to make it worthwhile.* We like to realize enough profit out of the deal up front so that if worst comes to worst and our buyer defaults, even if we never saw another penny from that deal, we would still feel we had a victory. Obviously, if your buyer defaults, you will move to get your money, oftentimes by foreclosing. Still, you can protect your peace of mind by always knowing you made enough that you are comfortable saying, "Next."

Once you've decided to sell with owner financing, you need to know how to protect yourself. To do this, you are going to use a few simple tools. The first tool you'll use is a *wraparound mortgage* or *all-inclusive trust* deed (AITD). As you learned in Chapter 2, a mortgage and a deed of trust are security instruments that ensure a borrower lives up to all the terms and conditions of a loan. The borrower signs a promissory note, which is evidence of the debt, and either a mortgage or deed of trust to secure the debt depending on which state the property is located in. A wraparound mortgage or AITD is a specialized version of an ordinary mortgage or deed of trust. We will go into more detail soon, but first remember when you learned about buying property "subject to" the existing financing how you can just take over making the payments on the loan. Just as you can buy "subject to" the existing financing, you can also sell "subject to" the existing financing. If you do this, you want to protect yourself if your buyer does not live up to the terms and conditions of the underlying loan and mortgage or deed of trust. You want to make sure your buyer maintains the property, keeps the property insured, pays the taxes, and makes the monthly payments on time.

If you sold the property "subject to" the existing financing without using the techniques in this section, you'd be powerless to stop your buyer from defaulting on the terms of the loan. You would no longer have any stake or say in the matter. To give yourself the power to force your buyer to comply, use a document called a wraparound mortgage or AITD. This is an additional document by which you can legally obligate your buyer to honor all the terms and conditions of the existing financing. In essence, it says that the buyer agrees to live up to all the terms and conditions of the existing financing, plus the buyer will pay back to you any money you carried back from the buyer's purchase of the property from you.

For example, imagine you bought a house for $300,000 with $10,000 down and "subject to" an existing $290,000 first mortgage. You decide to sell that house on a wraparound mortgage. The house is worth $330,000 to a cash buyer, but you know that if you offer nonbank financing, it's worth more. You find a buyer who's willing to buy from you for $350,000 with $35,000 down. To protect yourself, you get your buyer to sign a wraparound mortgage (if you live in a deed of trust state, then you would have the buyer sign an AITD, which acts just like a wraparound mortgage), securing that the buyer will not only pay you the rest of the money owed but will also live up to the terms and conditions of the first mortgage.

Many investors will have the buyer pay them one payment each month, and they will pay a portion of that payment to cover the existing first mortgage payment. In our previous example, if your buyer agreed to pay you interest-only payments at 9 percent on the $315,000 that you carried back, you would collect $2,362.50 each month from your buyer. With this money, you'd be obligated to pay the mortgage payment on the first mortgage of $2,000 a month. The extra $362.50 is yours to keep as one of your profit centers.

You could have your buyer pay the $2,000 directly to the first mortgage lender and then send you a second check for $362.50 each month, but we don't recommend it. While it's more work to collect the larger check and send the $2,000 to the existing first mortgage lender, you know your buyer is paying that mortgage on time. We suggest you collect the full payment of $2,362.50 and use that money to pay the first mortgage. If your buyer doesn't pay one month, then you won't pay the first mortgage, and you will immediately get a local attorney or foreclosure service to start the foreclosure. You can be nice and work with the buyer on the phone to find a solution. But any solution you work toward will have the deadline of the ticking foreclosure clock. Explain that it's not your decision to do it this way; it's your partner's choice. You're the "good cop" trying to find a way out, but you can't stop the "bad cop" (your partner) from moving forward with the fore-closure unless you receive payment of what is owed.

■ Success Team—Coach Mike's Story

I've found the best way to protect myself is to always start an eviction or foreclosure as soon as my renter or buyer has defaulted. While I'm empathetic and nice, I don't stop until I either get the property back or get payment in full. I guarantee you'll hear a million stories if you allow excuses. I urge you to set this firm policy, explain it to your renters and buyers up front, then hold them accountable to this specific standard. Anytime I have deviated from this in the past, I've regretted it.　■

Using Land Contracts when Selling with Owner Financing

A land contract (also known as a *bond for deed, agreement for deed,* or *contract for deed*) is another way to protect yourself when you sell with owner financing. A *land contract* is an installment sale by which you sell a property to a buyer who gets equitable title while you keep legal title. What's the difference? Not much. Equitable title means the buyer owns the property and gets to live in the house, write off all the deductions on tax forms, sell the property, etc. The buyer just isn't named on *legal title* (i.e., having the property *deeded* to them).

Think about it this way. When you buy a car from a dealer and the dealer finances the sale, you get to drive the car off the lot (equitable title). But the dealer's name is on the *pink slip* (legal title). When you pay off the entire loan, the dealer signs over the pink slip to you. If you default on the loan, the dealer takes back the car.

A land contract is essentially like a wraparound mortgage or AITD except that, in several states, it's easier to get the property back in the event your buyer defaults than if you sold the property on a wraparound mortgage or AITD. For example, in Ohio if your buyer has less than 10 percent equity in a property and defaults on the terms of the land contract, you can actually evict the buyer from the property. This process takes a few weeks. If you sold the property on a wraparound mortgage, it could take you months to go through Ohio's judicial foreclosure process.

In some states, however, selling on a land contract is a bad idea because of the difficulties posed to the seller trying to foreclose on a defaulting buyer. In California, for example, if you sold on a land contract, you would have to start a "quiet title action" lawsuit to extinguish your buyer's ownership interest before you could take the next step and evict the buyer from the property. You are much better off in California selling on an AITD.

Ask a *good* real estate attorney how land contracts versus wraparound mortgages or AITDs measure up in your state. The real key will be which way it's easier for you to get the property back or force the sale of the property if your buyer defaults. Ask your attorney the legal process you would need to follow if your buyer defaults. Then compare this process to the one you would need to go through if you sold the house on a wraparound mortgage or AITD. The bottom line is: if you ever sell with owner financing "subject to" the existing financing, *always* use either a wraparound mortgage or AITD or a land contract to protect your interest.

■ **Success Team—Commercial Coach Stephen's Story**

Recently an email was forwarded to me about how one of our students in Colorado, Larry, just sold a house on an installment land contract. Larry's wife found a seller who was three payments behind on his mortgage. Larry bought the house for $226,000, "subject to" the existing financing. He quickly refinanced the house to drop his payment to $1,405 PITI. He then put an ad in the paper and found a couple who wanted to buy the house from him for $250,000. They gave him $10,000 down and will pay him $2,066 each month. This gives Larry $661 of hassle-free income every month.   ■

SELLING WITH OWNER FINANCING

Marketing the Property

Let's say you have decided to sell your investment property with owner financing. Your first step is to market the property and generate as many prospective buyers as possible.

■ **Success Team—Coach Robb's Story**

In my opinion, the single most important factor in selling a house fast is to create intense competition for the property. Most investors struggle with this; they are slow to market the property. Yet there's power behind the urgency you create when selling a house.

The first two weeks it's on the market are critical. I'm a big believer in group showings with as many people as I can get to the property at the same time. This means I don't try to overqualify or sell the house over the phone. Instead, I push everyone who's remotely interested in the property to come see the house at the same time. I love the way buyers behave so nicely and decide so quickly when they fear losing the house to another family at the showing. ■

Besides placing signs, running ads in your local paper's real estate classified For Sale section is the best way to find a buyer for your property. Building on the classified advertising techniques you learned in the last chapter, Figure 8.2 offers three power ads you can use as templates when you're selling a property with owner financing.

FIGURE 8.2 *Power Ads When Selling a House with Owner Financing*

EZ Qualifying! OWC. Must sell now!
Price Reduced for Quick Sale.
3br/2ba, dbl gar. 619-555-1234.

OR

Desperate, Must Sell! $25,000 down take over pymts.
on my loan. No banks to deal with. 4br/3ba.
888-444-1212. 24-hr. rec. msg.

OR

Nonbank Financing! Bad Credit OK! Small down payment
with owner to carry entire balance! 3br./2.5ba. house.
Details call 888-444-1212 ext. 44. 24-hr. rec. msg.

Notice that each of these ads almost ignores the property and instead sells the financing. This is the same technique that car dealerships use when they advertise. They don't focus on the price; instead, they emphasize the payment and the amount of money needed up front.

You might be wondering where the price is in these ads. We recommend you *don't* include the price. Instead, use your ad to drive as many prospective buyers as possible to your recorded voice-mail message. Just as the purpose of your classified ad is to generate the phone call, the purpose of your voice-mail message is to get a caller to communicate contact information and the monthly payment range and down payment.

Sample Voice-Mail Script for Selling with Owner Financing

Hello, and thanks for calling. This is your chance to quickly and easily own your dream home. Right now we have a beautiful 4-bedroom, 2-bath home in Briargate. This home has a stunning view of the mountains and a great yard with a deck; it's very close to shopping and is on a quiet cul-de-sac.

We're offering this home with long-term owner financing. There are no banks to deal with and no long forms to fill out! This is the simplest and easiest way for you to own your own home.

To help us help you, after the tone, leave your name and telephone number, along with the range you want to keep your monthly payments in and the amount of down payment you have to work with. Obviously, the larger the monthly payments you can handle and the larger the down payment you have to work with, the easier it will be for us to choose you to buy this house.

Thanks for calling and remember to leave your name, telephone number, monthly payment, and down payment you have to work with, and if it's a match, we'll call you back as soon as we're back in the office.

Signs—Your Most Effective Source of Buyers

Whether you're selling the house on a rent-to-own basis or with owner financing, signs are one of the most important ways to attract qualified buyers to the property. Again, as recommended in the previous chapter, use a combination of two professional-looking signs in the front yard and the corner lot along with plain handwritten signs on simple poster board or corrugated plastic sheets. (See Figure 8.3.)

FIGURE 8.3 *Sample Neighborhood Sign to Sell with Owner Financing*

> No Bank Qualifying!
> 100% Owner Carry!
> 4bd./2ba. House
> 888-222-8488 ext. 45
> 24-hr. Rec. Msg.

■ **Mentor Family—Heidi's Story**

I received a deposit and a promise of $8,000 in option money from a couple who saw one of my bandit signs (the first sign that I ever put out, as a matter of fact). The man said he was driving to a Lowe's store when he caught sight of a tired-looking little yellow sign on a stake by the side of the road. The sign was curled up and flopped over so all he could read was "rent" and "3 bed." He said he got out of his car, went over to the sign, and held up the corners so he could read the whole thing. He got out his cell phone and punched in the toll-free number right there. So I guess these signs really do attract the attention of people in the market for a new place! ■

When you're using signs in a city or area that doesn't allow signs, try putting your signs out Friday afternoon before everyone drives home from work or very early on Saturday morning. If you remove them by Sunday night, you'll usually be able to avoid those people who don't like your signs as much as you do. In some areas, using your own wooden stakes or metal sign holders seems to relax the officials. One added benefit of handmade signs on poster board is that city authorities tend to see them as one-time events from harmless homeowners, not products of huge real estate investment firms (if only they knew, right!).

Your city probably does have rules about the use, or even against the use, of these signs. Because of that, we're not telling you to use signs; we're merely sharing that other investors have used signs to make a lot of money. You'll have to make your own autonomous decision after talking with your attorney, CPA, insurance agent, and psychologist. (How's that for a disclaimer?)

Flyers—Your Ace in the Hole

One powerful guerrilla-marketing technique to generate leads on prospective buyers is using flyers advertising the property for sale. You can deliver these flyers to homes in the surrounding neighborhood. (See Figure 8.4.) Don't forget to look for other

FIGURE 8.4 *Sample Flyer to Find Buyers*

$500 Reward
Wanted: The Perfect Neighbor

We want you to have the perfect neighbor,
so you can help us to choose your neighbor!

That's right . . . if you can help us to find a great
person or family to move into this:
3-bedroom, 2-bath home at 345 Vista View Way
We'll pay you a "reward" of $500

It's available as:
Rent to own
Owner Carry Financing
Nonqualifying Financing
Call 866-555-1234. 24-hr. rec. msg.
or office 303-555-1234
www.RentToOwnDenver.com

places to post flyers such as grocery stores, major employers, community bulletin boards, your local coffeehouse, etc.

■ **Success Team—Commercial Coach Rob's Story**

I recommend you hire someone else to put out these flyers for you. If you really want to be successful as an investor, you need to understand the real value of your time. It's hard to earn $50 an hour, let alone $500 or more an hour, if you're doing activities you could pay someone else $10 to $15 an hour to do. ■

Setting Up a Realistic Marketing Time Line

■ **Success Team—Coach Robb's Story**

For those number crunchers who want the metrics, here's a snapshot of the numbers I see when I'm marketing my properties. I get a huge number of signs (40 to 60) out the first two weeks. I put them out immediately and replenish them early on Friday afternoon. (Actually, I hire someone to post them.) This gets me about 25 calls on average. Of these, six to eight potential buyers will show up to see the property.

Signs are critical to find buyers even with the calls your classified ads generate. Typically, I receive 30 to 40 calls from my ads over two weeks, of which eight to ten people will come see the property. This means I get 14 to 18 prospective buyers to see the property within the first three weeks I have it on the market.

I place a *big* emphasis on showing a house to large groups (even if only one or two of the people really are qualified). Normally it takes me two to four showings to fill a property, and I collect nonrefundable deposits to hold from an average of 75 people who don't end up buying in addition to the one deposit to hold I get from the person who does buy.

The key is to push hard to generate traffic through the house for the first two weeks. If I get busy and slow down, I lose momentum, which I feel is *critical* to selling a house. Prospective buyers do pick up on this. On these occasions, it takes me about four to six weeks on average to sell to a tenant-buyer (rent to own) or buyer (owner financing).   ∎

Two More Hidden Profit Centers in Your Owner-Financing Deals

Because most of the buyers you'll find for your owner-financing properties have poor credit, they'll be more than willing to pay an above-market interest rate if you provide them with the financing. Most of your financing will be at 6 percent to 8 percent, and you'll be able to charge your buyer 8.9 percent to 10.9 percent interest. This will leave you with a healthy spread in the interest rates.

For example, let's say you bought a house "subject to" its existing $200,000 first mortgage at an interest rate of 7 percent. Then you sell the house on a wraparound mortgage for $230,000 with a $30,000 down payment and an interest rate of 8.9 percent. Not only did you make your $30,000 from the down payment, but you now have a spread in the interest rates that earns you 1.9 percent on the entire $200,000 balance. That passive income flows to you each month.

Finally, depending on the underlying loan and the financing you structure for your buyer, you may have one more profit center—the spread in the amortization of the loans. Referring to the previous example, let's say the loan you took title "subject to" is paying down $150 each month (and the amount keeps growing). But the loan you made to your buyer is interest only. That means each month the underlying loan is getting paid off and down the road will be much lower than $200,000. For example, in five years, your buyer may refinance the loan you made of $200,000. At that point, the underlying loan may have paid down to $192,000. This means you have an extra $8,000 payday.

Six Things Top Investors Do to Sell Fast

Top investors use a wide variety of strategies to sell property fast, and among the most popular are the following six:

1. They stay in control during all phone conversations to set appointments. Successful investors firmly take charge right from the start.
2. They know how to *pack* a showing with 5 to 10 families or potential buyers. Remember, more is better.
3. They *love* collecting deposits and feel great about people giving them money. Being comfortable accepting money isn't something you can take for granted. It's a state of mind that can be cultivated over time.
4. They know it takes only one person to buy the property; they feel confident that if the monthly payment and up-front money are right and the house looks decent, they *will* find a buyer.
5. They *expect* to collect a deposit to hold the property on the spot. Real buyers put up or shut up. A promise from a buyer only means something if it's accompanied with cash.
6. They don't care if they find the *perfect* buyer at the absolute *top* monthly payment and price. They just want a *good* buyer who gives them money right away.

 ■ **Success Team—Coach Emily's Story**

I've gone through all the "Oh my gosh, am I really going to be able to find someone . . . Oh poor me, what if I can't . . . What if I have to make the payments for the next six months myself . . . or if the seller freaks out . . . Did I really buy this right. . . ." Provided you've done your homework and bought right, have faith you will find a buyer. That confidence is contagious to buyers. Keep saying to yourself over and over, like a mantra, "I'm only looking for one buyer."   ■

A Powerful Selling Strategy: Rent-to-Own into Owner-Carry Financing

One useful strategy is to combine selling a house on a rent-to-own basis with owner-carry financing. For example, we sold a four-bedroom house for $279,980 on a two-year rent-to-own basis. Our tenant-buyers paid us a $15,000 option payment and a monthly rent of $1,695. At the end of the two years, they still couldn't qualify to buy using conventional financing, but they really wanted the house. So we agreed to finance them ourselves by selling it to them on an AITD (the house was in California where this is the best way to protect yourself when selling "subject to" the existing financing). We bumped their price to $285,000, and they gave us $15,000 more money as a down payment. We charged them interest-only payments at 8.9 percent, which meant they paid $1,891.25 a month. We also set a deadline for them to refinance the property within two years of the sale, when a balloon note for the rest of the money came due.

If you choose this combined selling strategy, following are your benefits:

- *Less risk.* You only rent-to-own first and don't agree to the owner-carry financing until after the buyer has proven to be a good risk.
- *Lots of control for you.* You don't obligate yourself to sell with owner financing; you merely agree to talk it through toward the end of the rent-to-own option period.
- *Growing streams of monthly cash flow.* You'll get a lot more money each month from your buyers than the rent they

used to pay. Because, at this point, they are owners, they also get to write off the interest they pay on their taxes. This means the net cost to your buyer will usually be negligible.

- *You sell at the future price.* When you sell on a rent-to-own basis, you charge an inflated price. When you roll this rent-to-own property into owner-carry financing, you can again bump the price because this nonbank financing commands a premium in the marketplace.
- *It's easy to find people who want to buy a house like this.* There are many times more buyers for rent-to-own or owner-financed homes than for traditional properties.
- *You save thousands in real estate commissions.* You won't need an agent to help you find a buyer.

SEVEN SECRETS TO SELL YOUR PROPERTIES FAST!

We want to close this chapter with the following seven secrets to selling properties fast:

1. *Always set up group appointments.* Your time is too valuable to show a property to one person at a time. Leverage your time by setting up group appointments. In addition to saving you time, this helps you create intense competition for your properties, which means you'll get more for your properties and get it faster. Never underestimate the fear of loss as a motivating force in your buyer's mind. When he or she looks around the house and sees four other families there, you'll be amazed how quickly a prospective buyer can decide to buy.
2. *Always make a "definite appointment," not a "showing."* While group showings are the way you think about marketing the property, that language is not the most effective with prospective buyers. Instead, always set up a definite appointment

with a prospective buyer at a specific time. You then go on to set all your definite appointments at the exact same time!

3. *Always get to the property early.* You have too much riding on each group showing to leave anything to chance. Get to the property 30 minutes early and make sure it is ready to show. Turn on all the lights and then do any last-minute touch-ups to make the house warm and inviting.

4. *Always use lots of neighborhood signs.* Dollar for dollar, signs are your cheapest and most effective way to generate buyers for your properties. Don't settle for one or two signs; instead, get 30 to 40 signs up each week.

5. *Always use voice mail to screen potential buyers.* This protects your time and gives buyers a safe way to find out more about the property and your offer. It also lets you make sure you balance your investing with other areas of your life. Return calls when it's convenient for you.

6. *Never talk through the numbers on the phone; wait until the buyer comes to the property.* Talking through price on the phone with prospective buyers is a big mistake. Never let them make a decision without meeting them at the property. If they push you to go through the pricing, say, "You know what. I've had a huge response of people for the property, and I don't have time to go through the pricing with each of them individually. To be frank, I don't even have the final pricing done [which is true since the final pricing is done only after you collect all the money]. At this point, I'm just getting back to all the people who called me saying they wanted to see the property. I'm quickly sorting out who I want to meet at the property to show through the inside and decide if I even want to sell it to them. May I ask you a few more questions to see if it even makes sense for me to invite you out to see the inside of the property?" You'll be amazed at how nicely they'll behave when they hear you firmly say these words.

7. *Never, ever stop marketing a property until you get a nonrefundable cash deposit in your hand (certified funds preferred).* Buyers are only buyers when they have paid you money. Period. Promises mean nothing from a buyer. We know this sounds harsh, but it's the sum total of a lot of years of experience talking. The best insurance you'll ever have that a buyer will come through is never to stop marketing the property until you've received cash in hand.

We hope that you will learn to master the techniques presented in this chapter and in Chapter 7. Remember, you create equity when you buy right; you create cash profits when you master the art of selling your properties. Given time and practice, you can become outstanding at this critical skill.

9

PUTTING YOUR FORECLOSURE BUSINESS ON AUTOPILOT TO GENERATE PASSIVE INCOME

What if there were a way to automate your foreclosure business so that it consistently generated $5,000 to $50,000 a month of real estate cash flow? And what if, instead of your having to do all the work each month to earn this money, you could build your investing business so that the *business* did the work? You'd get to enjoy the cash flow without the day-to-day stress.

Have we got your attention now? We're sure we do.

When done the right way, investing in real estate can create an inflation-proof cash flow that will take care of you and your family forever. Let's get one thing abundantly clear, however. *Setting it up will take work.*

Using the ideas we are about to share with you and working part-time, it may take you as long as 10 years to build your real estate cash flow to the point where you can retire and live comfortably on it. Working full-time, you may be able to do it in less than half that time.

■ Success Team—Peter's Story

Over the years, I've built businesses that invested in fore-closures, single-family houses, apartment buildings, and large commercial real estate projects. I've bought everything from small, one-bedroom condos to large apartment complexes to land development deals. Remember, when I first got started, I was a 33-year-old mechanic with no formal education, no big business experience, and no knowledge of real estate. But within three and a half years, I became a millionaire. If I can do it, you can do it too.

In fact, it's my belief that there is no better vehicle for creating and enjoying your wealth than real estate. It's such a simple yet powerful wealth-creating force that the average person can become incredibly successful with investing. The key is to get started before you think you're totally ready—because you'll never feel *totally* ready!   ■

THE THREE INVESTOR LEVELS—YOUR PROVEN FAST TRACK TO REAL ESTATE SUCCESS

The three investor levels—your proven fast track to real estate investment success—are described in the sections below.

Level One

Level One investing is all about belief. It's about proving to yourself that not only does real estate work for other people, but that it works for *you*! How do you prove this to yourself? By *doing* a few deals and making a significant profit. As a Level One investor, you eventually gain the certainty that real estate will be your proven path to financial success. The key for Level One is getting yourself into action.

Level Two

Level Two investing is all about mastering the five core investor skills of real estate investing (see Figure 9.1) and building an investment business that works without your needing to run it day to day. At first, Level Two is about building your knowledge base of investing strategies, tools, and techniques. Later, it's about building a real estate investing *business.*

Building your knowledge base helps you leverage yourself. Building your investing *business* lets you leverage other people, systems, and outsourced solutions to create value in the marketplace without your being there to do the work.

Why is this so important for you? Because ultimately if you don't learn to leverage yourself through building a strong business infrastructure of systems and people, you'll be limited in two critical ways. First, you'll be limited in the scale of projects and profits you can earn; you just can't do big deals without the infrastructure in place to make the deal stand. Second, unless you build an investing business, you'll be limited in your potential to create the time and freedom you truly want. That's why it's so important to learn to build an investing *business.*

FIGURE 9.1 *The Five Core Skills of Successful Investors*

1. Marketing—Finding great deals in any market
2. Structuring—How to structure win-win real estate deals
3. Negotiation—How to get the other party to say *yes* to the deal you want
4. Analysis—How to determine if a deal is good in five minutes or less
5. Contracts—How to write up money-making real estate deals

Level Three

Level Three investing is all about transitioning into the role of a passive investor and business owner. If Level Two investors are the heart pumping their business forward, Level Three investors are the brain directing the big picture of the business and enjoying the consistent profits from that business, without getting caught up in any of the daily activities. Imagine having built your real estate miniempire in such a way that you earn massive income without directing the business day to day.

Level Three investors have simply learned to put their investing on autopilot so they don't just make money, but they create *passive* streams of income.

In the beginning, you'll have to front-load your effort as you develop as an investor. It will take you hundreds of units of effort to succeed as a Level One investor and get your first few paydays. Later, as a Level Two investor, it will take you 10 to 20 units of effort to get your paydays. And finally, as a Level Three investor, it may only take one or two units of effort to enjoy a lifetime of paydays. The secret is to understand that it really is worth getting all the way to Level Three, but that you've got to pay your dues to get started.

■ **Success Team—Commercial Coach Stephen's Story**

Once we understood how to market to and find homeowners behind in payments, how to negotiate debt with the bank, and the process of buying foreclosures, we then could create a system around short sales. We began to look at each home to determine the best exit strategy. This step is critical and often overlooked when purchasing a foreclosure home. Once you have negotiated with the bank, you need to have the funds to close the transaction. We learned early the art of double closings, fix and flip opportunities using soft or hard money, and how to use real estate agents to assist us in getting our properties onto the MLS.

The foreclosure business we created gave us the cash flow to venture into more aggressive Level Three investing. Without the cash flow that our foreclosure business provided, we would not have had the flexibility to look at more complex real estate investments. To this day, our foreclosure business is alive and thriving. We have turned that into a Level Three activity. We now have buyers we have trained to do the transactions, and we share in the profits. It keeps cash coming in and allows us to stay in our highest and best-use activities, which are now all in Level Three.   ■

Key Characteristics of a Level Three Foreclosure Business

Following is a list of the key characteristics of a foreclosure business operated at Level Three:

- It's healthy and growing yet takes fewer than 10 hours a month of your time.
- All day-to-day buying and selling decisions are based on proven formulas that are immune to individual opinions and mistakes.
- It has the capacity to take on more business without decreasing net profits.
- It's flexible enough to make money in any real estate market.
- It has comprehensive business systems documented in manuals, not merely in the heads of your team.
- It creates cash flow, long-term wealth, and a fun, balanced lifestyle for your team and for you, the owner.

Once you've taken action as a Level One investor, the next hurdle you'll face is succeeding as a Level Two investor who needs to refine his or her investing skills, then build an investing business.

Let's break this down into finer detail so you can use these insights to do what the average investor never does. You can free yourself from the day-to-day need to run your foreclosure business and reach Level Three success.

Three Stages of Level Two Investing

Level Two investing is broken down into three distinct stages. Each of these stages has a different developmental focus for you, the investor. Here's a quick snapshot of each of these stages.

Early Stage Level Two. If you are in this stage, you're learning to master the five core skills of successful investors: finding deals, structuring deals, negotiating deals, analyzing deals, and contracts and paperwork.

It usually takes Early Stage Level Two investors 12 months to learn the core skills and gain the confidence and composure to use those skills effectively. Once they've built this foundation of skills, they move on to Middle Stage Level Two investing.

Middle Stage Level Two. If you're in this stage, you are refining your investor skills and learning to leverage yourself so you can produce more for your investing business. At this point in your investing, you are the central hub around which your business revolves. You're like a doctor whose whole office is organized as efficiently as possible.

As a Middle Stage Level Two investor, you leverage your time every way you can by building the team and systems around you to keep producing for your business. You've become fluent in all five of the core investor skills. You can take a deal and work it smoothly from start to finish, troubleshooting it along the way as needed. With this competence comes the confidence to jump on good deals fast.

Yes, you're still working to fine-tune your five core investor skills, but at this point, it's much more about making small *refinements* than developing these skills from scratch. As you transition through Middle Stage Level Two investing, you increase the number of ways you leverage yourself by building systems and growing your investing team. You tentatively let go of pieces of your business and free up your time to focus on those parts that earn you the greatest return for the time and energy invested. You hire a full-time or part-time assistant, outsource your bookkeeping, and perhaps even contract with someone to show your properties (ideally on a commission basis where you only pay for results).

At this point, you either make the crucial shift to leverage yourself by growing your investing business, or you get caught in the daily grind of being the sole producer for your investing business. Many Middle Stage Level Two investors get trapped because they never learn to separate their business from themselves. Refining your skills and leveraging your time can make you an extremely successful Middle Stage Level Two investor, but ultimately to break out of the small-time bubble, you need to build an investing business that has a life beyond your being the hub of it.

As you know, you'll ultimately reach a limit to what you're able to produce through your own efforts. This is why it's important to progress to Advanced Stage Level Two investing.

Advanced Stage Level Two. You're building the systems, teams, and outsourced solutions your business needs to generate profits consistently and independently of you and your efforts.

As a Middle Stage Level Two investor, you were the central hub around which you built the pieces of a viable business. Chances are, you were the one driving it, negotiating the deals, and directing who does what (see Figure 9.2). The biggest difference between a Middle Stage Level Two and an Advanced Stage Level Two investor is that in the Middle Stage, you're building the business to complement *your* skills and leverage *your* investing efforts. But because you remain at the hub, if you aren't actively involved, your Middle Stage Level Two business will grind to a halt.

FIGURE 9.2 *5 Advanced Techniques to Leverage Yourself as an Investor*

Technique 1: Use "standardized" forms and contracts that you can complete quickly

Technique 2: Only perform your due diligence *after* you have the property under contract

Technique 3: Value your time—hire an assistant

Technique 4: Outsource to high-quality vendors in a way that lowers your real cost and provides greater results for you

Technique 5: Use technology to make it easy to get paid:
- Direct deposit
- Auto draft
- Payroll deduction

Later, when you transition to Advanced Stage Level Two investing, you will work toward replacing yourself in your investing business altogether. At that point, you'll fundamentally shift your focus from inwardly looking at yourself to outwardly focusing on your business.

What critical perspective shift leads to true financial freedom and security—and ultimately to a Level Three lifestyle? *It's to see yourself not as an investor but as a business creator* who is growing a real estate investing business that works without your being there to run it. You're there "creating" only until you can build a business that can replace yourself. In essence, you are the engineer, designing and building a profit machine that consistently kicks out a cash flow every month.

Many investors mistakenly believe their core goal is to become a skilled real estate investor. It's not. It's to build a *profitable investing business that makes you money without your being there to work the business actively.*

Let me remind you that the world is full of skilled landlords who spend their days dealing with leaky faucets and late-paying tenants. And it's full of skilled investors who frantically move from one deal to the next in the chaotic game of real estate. Those who are landlords may make consistent money with their investing, but they are chained to the obligations of managing their rental portfolio. Those investors who frantically move from deal to deal may make a lot of money, but they usually get stuck on the treadmill of having to find, close, and turn their next deal to keep the money flowing.

So as you build your foreclosure business, make sure you're building with the goal of having a viable business independent of you. When you've accomplished this, you transition into Level Three investing. You're not only financially free, but you're able to focus your time wherever you want.

Ultimately, if you want to be a Level Three investor enjoying a Level Three lifestyle, your business needs to be systems driven, not people dependent.

THREE KEYS TO WORK SMARTER AND BUILD YOUR LEVEL THREE FORECLOSURE BUSINESS

If you want to learn to work smarter and build your Level Three foreclosure business faster, you will need to master the following three key strategies.

First Key: Set Up Systems

The first key is to use powerful systems to help you get the results you want with less work and effort. A system is an organized process or tool that helps you and your team consistently produce an excellent result in an area of your business.

FIGURE 9.3 *The 12 Building Blocks of Great Business Systems*

1. Scripts
2. Worksheets
3. Spreadsheets with built-in formulas
4. Other software that automatically does steps or processes information for you
5. Databases of key information
6. Templates and samples
7. Common question and answer sheets
8. Step-by-step instructions
9. Predictable problem areas and how to deal with them
10. Camera-ready artwork available to use
11. Preapproved investor forms and contracts
12. A time line or master calendar

Systems can refer to a script of what to say, a checklist that lays out a procedure, a sample document, a spreadsheet of key information, or a worksheet to fill out (see Figure 9.3). *A system creates a shortcut to help any person on your team with little training get a desired result in a specific area.*

An example of this might be the "I Buy Houses" signs that you learned about in Chapter 4 on how to find profitable foreclosure deals. Your system for this marketing program might be a detailed checklist or spreadsheet that contains the following information:

- An explanation of how and where the signs are used in your business
- Reorder levels and vendors to order from
- Any standard or special pricing that you have negotiated. (You did negotiate a special price, didn't you?)

- Vendor websites, phone numbers, email addresses, and contact person(s)
- Specific sizes, colors, and words to go on the signs, including the correct toll-free number(s) to use
- Your shipping address and the credit card to bill
- Placement locations for your signs, including a log of how long the signs tend to stay in place

We advocate actually writing down all processes, step by tedious step. This will take effort on your and your team's part to build these systems, but you'll find the rewards worthwhile.

Ultimately to take your investing business as far as you want it to go, it will need to be systems driven, not people reliant. You never know when a key person will leave. So capture the most important knowledge about how to run your business successfully into clear, simple systems that guarantee healthy profits, year after year after year.

The best systems empower your team to produce exceptional results. They're not about control but rather about freedom. Using the right systems frees your team from worrying about details. They can keep a larger perspective and spot opportunities to tap into. All this will generate greater profits for your business.

Second Key: Specialized Knowledge

It's time to work smarter to gain the specialized knowledge you need to leverage results. What do you think makes skilled investors able to structure hugely profitable deals while beginning investors struggle with what they can do with their sellers? One thing and one thing only: *experience.*

That's the power of specialized knowledge. It can easily be borrowed from other successful investors without having to discover it yourself through trial and error.

Remember, you're not out to make yourself indispensable. You want to be able to transfer your skills, experience, and decision-making ability into your investing business so that the business out-produces you without your needing to be there to oversee it.

Third Key: Cohesive Action Plan

One of the most costly myths in the world of investing is that the best investors "fly by the seat of their pants" and "go purely on intuition."

The opposite is true. The best investors have clear action plans that tie together all their investing activities. Having your own business plan allows you to decide intelligently to step *off* of the plan to take advantage of an unexpected opportunity when you see it. The best investors understand the power of quickly seizing an unplanned opportunity and have the ability to improvise to leverage opportunities for maximum gain with minimum work and risk. They can quickly modify their individual action plan to accommodate a new opportunity and tie it into the larger goals of their investing business.

As you grow your foreclosure business, it's critical that you consistently upgrade your business plan to take into account both lessons you're learning and changing market conditions. In this way, you'll stay nimble, flexible, and focused—the core ingredients of a successful foreclosure business.

■ **Success Team—Peter's Story**

I used to fight this change a lot. I thought, "How could anyone negotiate better than me? How could anyone handle the closing paperwork better than me? How could anyone oversee the reselling of the property better than me?" The truth is that once I built my investing business, I was freed from all of these areas. When I became an advisor and coach to those who actually did all the steps in the deal, my income skyrocketed. It allowed me to step back from my investing to sort through bigger-picture decisions strategically about which projects to take on next.

I make many times more money from my investing today than I ever did, and I spend on average fewer than 10 hours a month engaged in managing each of my investing businesses. Now, I point the businesses in the right direction, help make the decision to pull the trigger on the next deal, then check in from time to time to coach my team on making deals go better or improve the systems so they run even smoother. This is the most fulfilling part of building my investing business—this freedom to make a leveraged difference by having the time and space to see the entire business from the outside looking in.   ■

Seven Steps to Building a Business System

While there are many, many steps in building any business system, the seven described below may be the most important.

Step One: Clearly define the outcome or desired result for the system under construction. What do you want the business system to do? What result do you want it to produce consistently?

Step Two: Find the best person in your business (or outside your business if you have access to someone better) to model your business system on. Whom do you know who is world-class professional in an area of your investing business that you could model?

Step Three: Observe them producing the result and freeze them as they progress to write down each of the steps they take and the order in which they take them. Whether it's yourself or another person, follow the progress as a highly skilled person produces the result you want the business system to produce. List the steps this person takes and the order in which they're taken.

Step Four: Repeat step three a few times to make sure you have mastered all the steps and their exact order. With complicated business processes that involve interactions with others, you'll likely take several times through to get a draft of all the steps down accurately. Each time you go through the process, you're fine-tuning your documentation of the process and procedure.

Step Five: Teach the system to new people and see if they can use it to achieve the desired outcome. Nothing shows the weaknesses and holes of a system better than getting a new person to try out the system. By watching the learning process, it's easy to spot the steps that you didn't write down earlier. You'll also be able to spot the steps that need more explanation.

Step Six: Make the system even easier to use by filling in the gaps with checklists, instructions, worksheets, scripts, samples, etc. The best way to see where the gaps are is to pay attention to the questions and struggles of the team members you're training. It's their fresh, new perspective that will give you accurate feedback on where to beef up the system.

Step Seven: Simplify the system and refine it over time. See what steps of the system could be automated by building the right software or worksheet. How could you eliminate or combine steps? Is there a simpler way to get the desired results? You should not only be building systems over time, but you should also be *pruning* your existing systems so they stay fresh, healthy, and vibrant. *Your goal is to get more from less.* Sometimes the best tool you can use in your foreclosure business isn't a pen or a hammer but an eraser.

10

PUTTING IT ALL
INTO ACTION

Over the past nine chapters, you've learned the nuts and bolts of how to make money investing in fore- closures. You've learned 12 ways to structure deals without cash or credit and 22 ways to find great foreclosure deals. You've learned a simple five-step system to close deals with sellers in foreclosure and how to avoid the 24 most common foreclosure pitfalls. Finally, you've learned how to convert your foreclosure deals into either quick cash or long-term wealth.

The fact is, your head is probably bursting with moneymaking ideas by this point. Now it's time to turn your attention to the best way to translate all this specialized knowledge into money in your pocket. Following is a seven-step action plan to launch your foreclosure investing business, with each one explained:

1. Test three different lead sources
2. Meet with three sellers as fast as you can
3. Dive in and learn how to invest the right way
4. Establish three to five secure lead sources

5. Meet with two to four sellers a week, every week
6. Start cultivating sources of funding
7. Constantly learn and grow from your experiences

STEP ONE: TEST THREE DIFFERENT LEAD SOURCES

Go back to Chapter 4 and choose any three lead sources to try. Your goal (in this and in the next step) isn't to sign up deals but to get a feel for what the real world of investing is like. Over the course of two or three weeks, use these three trial runs to find three sellers you can meet with to practice your negotiating skills. Remember, you're testing the waters at this stage so you can ease into your investing.

STEP TWO: MEET WITH THREE SELLERS AS FAST AS YOU CAN

Now that you've found a few sellers who might be motivated, meet with them. You probably feel you're not even close to taking this step. You'll say that you don't know enough or you're not ready. Do it anyway!

Your immediate goal is to experience what it *feels* like to be sitting face-to-face with a real live seller. Do you know that many would-be investors have spent years studying how to invest without ever taking this critical step of *meeting* with a seller? Remember, no matter how much you learn about investing, you're still going to feel scared and overwhelmed during your first few appointments. Knowing this, just get these appointments over with so you can get on with the business of learning to make money with your investing.

To put you at ease, we don't expect you to buy any of these houses. (Of course, you can if you want to.) In fact, to take all the pressure off, you can even visit with these sellers deciding beforehand that you are *not* going to buy any of the properties. The point is to prove *to yourself* that you can meet with sellers and survive. Once this step is out of the way, the rest comes easily. Now, when you commit to this stage, you'll have real experience with which to make sense out of what you're learning.

STEP THREE: DIVE IN AND LEARN HOW TO INVEST THE RIGHT WAY

One of our favorite quotes is, "If you think education is expensive, you should try ignorance." At this point, you have a better understanding of what's needed, so it's time to get busy. While no university degrees exist for making money as an investor, if you're willing to take responsibility for your real estate education, you can create a self-study program tailored to your needs and goals.

One word of caution: Make sure you're learning only from the best. Edward Deming, the world's foremost quality control expert, repeatedly said there's a precious window of opportunity to train someone to do things the right way from the start. He cautioned businesses to make sure they either used their best people or brought in the best people to train their staff because if people don't learn something right at the beginning, it's much harder to get them to unlearn what they know and change their patterns.

We recommend you pay the price and learn how to invest the right way from the start. Take great care to model your actions after people who are the best in the world at what they do. We've provided a detailed list of resources for you to tap into to learn more about how to make money investing at the end of the book.

You have the following five powerful sources to learn from:

1. *Books.* It takes an author five years or more of experience and study to gather the insights to put into a book that you can read in a few weeks. This is a great form of leverage.

■ Success Team—Coach Robb's Story

People might call me a bookworm, and that's fine by me. I read 125 books or more each year. Not only do I love to learn, but the ideas I harvest from this intensive study have helped me make millions of dollars. ■

2. *Home study courses.* The next step up from learning by books is carefully to complete several high-quality home-study courses. These courses usually include audio training (using time-coded CDs is preferable because it's easy to go straight to the area you want to review), video components, and a detailed manual. The most important aspect about a home study course is how *current* and *detailed* it is. A quality home study course should not just tell you *what* to do, but specifically *how* to do it. A benefit to today's high-tech culture is being able to transfer high-quality content onto your computer and your MP3 player in minutes and listen to it whenever and wherever you want. My coaches and I have hundreds of audio books and home study courses on our iPods™ and have found this to be a convenient and fun way to grow our knowledge base.

■ Success Team—Peter's Story

I didn't go to college. In fact, I struggled to make it out of high school. I regard my investment in home study courses as my college education. The only difference is that the courses I chose weren't at all theoretical—they were down-to-earth guides that came from my instructor's real-world experiences. Because I'm an auditory person, I learn best by listening to material. That's why I am constantly upgrading my knowledge base by listening to my iPod™ through my car's stereo system when I'm driving and on my portable player when I'm exercising. Considering that most successful investors I know out-earn college graduates by a factor of 10 on average, I'd say this kind of investment can pay off handsomely. ∎

3. *Workshops.* There is something powerful about shutting out the world and immersing yourself in an intensive learning environment for several days straight. In fact, many people can learn in a few days what other investors struggle for years to learn. So consider attending one or two high-quality real estate workshops each year as part of your ongoing investing education. Also, see if you can purchase the audio and video recordings of the workshop to review later. Considering the amount of material you'll be exposed to at most workshops, you'll benefit immensely by repeating the course several times.

4. *Investor associations.* The power of association is such a strong driving force to help you succeed as an investor that we recommend harnessing it to help you reach your goals faster. Get in touch with the investor associations in your areas and start attending their meetings and networking with the most successful investors in the group. (See the resources listed at the back of the book for details on finding an investor association in your area. For a listing of websites to find an investor association near you, see Appendix B.)

5. *Mentors.* The word *mentor* derives from Greek and means a trusted friend, counselor, or teacher, usually a more experienced person. The fastest way to succeed at investing (or anything else) is to find a successful person or team that is willing to take you by the hand and guide you. Following are five questions you'd be wise to ask of any foreclosure mentoring program to find the best fit:

   • *Question One: How big is the mentoring program?* Some people prefer working with the largest companies, which have tens of thousands of clients. Other people prefer working with an individual they know who informally works with just one or two people at a time. Many of our clients choose us because they get the best of both worlds. We work only with a small number of clients each year (currently around 1,000) so we can give them individual attention. But we have a large enough investor pool that we constantly get exposed to new and innovative ideas to share with our clients around the country. The key is to choose the right size of program or group for you.

- *Question Two: Who does the actual coaching?* Make sure you find out exactly who will do the actual mentoring. Some programs use staff members as full-time coaches who are available from 9:00 AM to 5:00 PM. While convenient, these "full-time" coaches rarely are full-time investors; rather, they are simply semitrained employees.

■ Success Team—Peter's Story

Several years ago, we decided that the coaches we'd use would come up through the ranks of our program. This helped ensure that their investing philosophy as well as practice would be consistent with what we taught. We also insisted that they have the heart to give back to our students. This meant we use only full-time investors as part-time coaches. While this really limits the number of people we can work with because they only coach on a part-time basis, we still decided this was the best way to train our clients. ■

- *Question Three: How much access to coaching will you really get?* Make sure you investigate all the ways you can get your questions answered. Also ask these questions: How does the program use technology to make it easier for you to obtain quality help? How long does your support last? You want the program to give you at least six months of support, preferably a full year or longer.

- *Question Four: Is there a system in place?* A system is the sum total of a business' methods and procedures—that business' best practices and working processes in one place. Take a close look to make sure a strong match exists between the system offered and your desired outcome.
- *Question Five: Will you be held accountable?* Whenever people are doing something new or different, it can be too easy for them not to follow the behavior that will lead them to success. That's why we hold our students accountable for their behavior, even going as far as having them submit weekly performance summaries. While you don't need to find a program that goes that far, it's essential to find a program that won't let you slide by but will hold you to your commitments as an investor heading to the bank.

■ **Mentor Family—John's Story**

I got off to a blazing start with my own investing career. After spending time with Peter, my mentor who showed me how to negotiate with sellers, I went after investing in a big way. I remember a point early in my career when I got nine properties under contract in the same month. But I became so scared, I hid in my house. For two weeks, I was so overwhelmed by the "success" I'd already had, I didn't call a single seller I had a pending deal with, nor did I market a single property. As you probably guessed, I lost a lot of those deals because the sellers got scared when I disappeared. In the end, we closed on only one of those nine properties.   ■

We require every student who signs up to work through a 29-point checklist to find the end user for their property with one of our coaches. One of the reasons is that it's too easy to let fear cause you to procrastinate or hide. Matching up with the right mentor or team can shorten your learning curve by several years.

In fact, it's often the single greatest leverage point to succeed quickly when investing in foreclosures.

STEP FOUR: ESTABLISH THREE TO FIVE SECURE LEAD SOURCES

About three weeks into your study phase, you will actually start investing. You will not feel totally ready, but do it anyway. Your goal is to test systematically different lead-generating sources until you find three to five that will each yield, on average, one high-quality lead a week. While it might take you several months to establish these independent lead sources, once you have them, your investing business will be on a rock-solid foundation. To be successful with your investing, you'll need access to motivated sellers, and this takes work.

STEP FIVE: MEET WITH TWO TO FOUR SELLERS A WEEK, EVERY WEEK

You must meet with a lot of sellers to find good deals. At first, you'll be working on getting comfortable being in their homes. Soon, you'll relax enough to stop thinking about what you are going to say next and actually *listen* to what these sellers are sharing with you. Next, you'll get good at quickly analyzing a deal and knowing what you could offer the seller that will meet his or her needs and make you a fair profit. Finally, you'll master the art of the end game—of closing the deal.

This is a progression; the only known path to success is meeting with enough sellers to work through this process. Once you master your skills and become good at all these stages, you'll be able to earn a whole lot more money with less time and effort. So commit to meeting consistently with sellers to make this happen.

STEP SIX: START CULTIVATING SOURCES OF FUNDING

Once you've paid your dues and learned enough to sign up a deal or two, start to cultivate some outside funding sources. Begin with brainstorming a list of all the people you know who might know others who want to earn a healthy rate of return on any idle cash they may have. Because any of these loans will be secured by a mortgage on a property with a lot of equity protecting this private lender, this will be a safe investment for them.

Also, see about establishing any lines of credit at your local bank. Talk with your bank about creating an equity line of credit. While you might choose not to use these sources of funding, it's a good idea to establish them early just in case. It's always easier to borrow money when you *don't* need it.

Next, find out who the hard moneylenders are in your area. Ask around at your local real estate investors association meeting or look in the newspapers under "Money to Lend" or "Real Estate Wanted." Call people in these categories to find out their requirements for lending you money, then start to cultivate relationships with them.

Finally, put together your investors list of people you can flip deals to in case you find some deals you can't fund yourself. This is the easiest way to create a quick cash flow with your investing. Review Chapter 7 to refresh your memory about how to create this list.

STEP SEVEN: CONSTANTLY LEARN AND GROW FROM YOUR EXPERIENCES

With all this investing activity going on, make sure you profit from every step you take. Ask yourself every week, "What have I learned so far from these investing experiences?" Capture on paper the tangible learning points you've gathered that week from investing. What's been working well for you? What are you most pleased about in your investing? What are the biggest questions you need answers to? What can you do differently next week as a result of what you learned this week that will create the most dramatic, positive impact on your investing?

One powerful technique you can harness is called *masterminding*. A mastermind group brings together two or more people for a definite purpose, in a spirit of mutual harmony and trust, in a manner in which every member benefits. That's a mouthful! Bottom line is that a mastermind group of three to five other investors meets regularly to assist each other in becoming successful with their investing. They'll give you objective input and encouragement to supercharge your investing, and you'll do the same for them.

TITHING AND SEEDING—GETTING COMFORTABLE WITH WEALTH

When you become comfortable with being wealthy, you happily do these two things: (1) give some of your money to good causes and (2) plant seeds for a flourishing future. Let's explain these concepts more fully.

Tithing: Giving Part of What You Earn to the Greater Good

Perhaps the most significant distinction we can share with you is the difference between being wealthy and being rich. Being rich means you have money, but we bet you know several people who have a truckload of money but aren't happy. Either they're scared to death of losing their money so they hold on to it with a tight, white-knuckled grip, or their relationships with others are distant and unfulfilling. You get the picture.

Being wealthy means having abundance in all areas of your life—physical, financial, emotional, and spiritual. We want you to transform your life in a way that includes much more than just a big bank account.

An important aspect of being wealthy is feeling like you have *more than enough.* This feeling of abundance only comes from having so much that you can congruently say you have more than you need. And there's no stronger affirmation that you truly have more than you need than to give some of it away.

We recommend you decide on a percentage of your real estate earnings to give away in a manner that makes a positive difference in the world. Whether you call this tithing or just paying for your space on planet earth, it's the most powerful way to shift your thinking to *knowing* you live in an abundant world and that you *are* wealthy. It doesn't matter what percentage you choose to give away (we think 10 percent is a good number); all that matters is that you do choose to give something away.

Many of us accumulated so much negative input about what it means to have money that we're scared or uncomfortable or ashamed to allow it to flow into our lives. So by giving part of what you earn to the greater good, you also recondition your mind about what it means to have money. It simply means you can do a lot of good in the world.

Seeding: Investing in What Matters Most

In addition to giving a percentage of your real estate profits to worthy causes, we recommend investing a portion of your profits in the three areas described below. We call this *seeding.* You know how some farmers set aside a small portion of their harvest to use as seeds for the next season? Similarly, seeding is investing in areas you'll use to make sure you live in a wealthy way all the seasons of your life. Take care to set aside the money out of your profits today so your tomorrow will be even more rewarding and secure.

1. *Invest in assets that grow.* Take a definite percentage of your real estate profits and set them aside to invest in other real estate deals. Over time, your goal is to create an asset base of properties that generates multiple streams of passive income.

2. *Invest in your earning capacity.* Take a definite percentage of your real estate profits and invest them in your ongoing real estate education. One of your greatest appreciating assets is your ability to make more money with your investing.

3. *Invest in your relationships.* Take a definite percentage of your real estate profits and use it to create experiences of joy and connection with your loved ones. Use the money for a vacation with your family, take your spouse on a special date, or do something else out of the ordinary. Find ways to create special moments and memories with the people who matter most to you.

What has all this got to do with making money investing in foreclosures? Everything! Until you are able to hardwire into your brain the message that "making money is a good thing" and "you use your wealth in positive and uplifting ways," we believe you can never truly be wealthy. Tithing and seeding are powerful life choices to help you reach your goal of achieving true wealth.

IT'S REALLY POSSIBLE FOR YOU

We've come to the end of our time together in this book, which means it's time for you to step out and put into practice what you've been learning. We know it can feel overwhelming and scary, but just keep in mind it's not real—it just *feels* real.

Remember the story about that investor from Colorado named Byron? He got started as a full-time investor after being laid off from his high-paying job as a corporate sales manager. For the first four months of his investing, he didn't close any deals. About that time, he and his wife were looking at their depleted savings and wondering if Byron should just go and find another job.

Then a small "accident" changed their lives. Byron came across a copy of *Making Big Money Investing in Real Estate Without Tenants, Banks, and Rehab Projects* at a local bookstore. Something about that book and the ideas in it sparked him to try things a new way. One month later, Byron joined our Mentorship program, and three weeks after the live training portion, he signed up his first deal. In fact, a week after that, he picked up his *second* deal. Over the next six months, Byron went on to complete nine deals, made $75,000 cash, and created more than $200,000 of equity for himself and his wife. He also created a $2,000 passive monthly cash flow from his investment properties. He's moved on to many more deals. If Byron can do this, it's possible for you, too.

Or take Mike, a student who has been blind for the past six years. Mike sent us an email about a house he bought "subject to" the existing financing from a seller in foreclosure. He made $20,000 profit. If Mike can do this, know that you can, too. You just need to take action and go after your dreams.

Or take Scott, a laid off IT manager who took the plunge to begin investing in foreclosures. Scott struggled in the first year of his investing before he hit his stride. Since then, he's completed more than 20 deals and has a thriving investing business. He says one of the best parts to his investing is that he can plan his work around his family, not the other way around. Can you think of any greater gift to give *your* family?

■ Success Team—Peter's Story

I remember when I bought my first fourplex from a seller who responded to my classified ad. My ad read, "Private investor wants income property. Will look at all. Any condition." The sellers, an elderly couple, had just foreclosed on the property when their previous buyer had stopped making payments. I was so scared when I talked with them over the phone, my hands were shaking. I remember sitting with them on their back porch and pouring out my dreams of becoming a real estate investor. I'm sure I did it all wrong, but somehow these two generous spirits took a chance on me and sold me the property with owner financing. The $87,000 I made when I sold that property four years later was less important to me than the powerful experience of this couple's believing in me *when I didn't have the courage to believe in myself.* ■

Know that the Success Team and our entire Mentor Family believe in you. We *know* you can do this. It's not just possible . . . it's possible for *you*!

We wish you true wealth and lasting happiness.

~Peter Conti

A

YOUR FORECLOSURE BONUS WEB PACK—

A Free $245 Gift From Peter and the Success Team

As our way of congratulating you for finishing this book, we've set up a special bonus pack of all kinds of investor goodies on a special website. Because we have so much more we want to share with you about investing in foreclosures but ran out of space here, we've placed all this extra material on the website for you.

FOLLOWING IS WHAT YOU'LL GET WHEN YOU CLAIM YOUR BONUS WEB PACK

- A state-by-state simple summary of the foreclosure process
- Links to the applicable state laws for many areas of the country investors must know about
- Free access to Peter's "Secrets to Short Sales with Foreclosures" training
- How to get investor-friendly forms and contracts
- "How to Protect Your Assets" guide for investors

- A *free* one-year subscription to *The Success Team Investor's Tips E-Newsletter*
- Short sale packet sample download

AUDIO INTERVIEWS WITH LEADING FORECLOSURE EXPERTS

Also, as part of your Bonus Web Pack, you'll receive free access to more than *six hours* of downloadable foreclosure training! You'll meet some of the nation's leading foreclosure experts as they share their best ideas on how you can be more successful.

Following is just some of what you'll learn from these powerful sessions:

- How one ex-IBM accountant earned a seven-figure investment income handling more than 30 rehab projects a year—and how you can, too
- How one real estate entrepreneur made more than $1 million in less than three years investing in foreclosures with private lenders—and how you can, too

You'll also have access to 12 special audio sessions with Peter walking you through foreclosure secrets that build on what you've learned from this book.

HOW YOU GET YOUR BONUS WEB PACK FOR FREE

To get your *free* Bonus Web Pack, simply go to *www.ForeclosureBonusPack.com*. When you're at this site, you'll be asked to register, so when asked for your "entry code," type in **46book**. This will give you complete access to your Bonus Web Pack.

ONE MORE FREE GIFT FOR REGISTERING WITHIN 30 DAYS OF BUYING THIS BOOK

For a limited time only, you'll be able to download the following two free special reports:

- Report One: "The 27 Questions You Must Ask Before You Purchase Any Foreclosure"
- Report Two: "The Inside Secrets of the San Diego Challenge: How a Group of Three Beginning Investors Picked Up $1.5 Million Worth of Real Estate with Only $37 Down"

Thank you for buying and reading this book. Good luck with your investing and the life transformations that are sure to happen as a result!

Peter Conti

P.S. To get your *free* Bonus Web Pack ($245 value), simply go to *www.ForeclosureBonusPack.com* and register using the entry code **46book**.

B

RESOURCES TO HELP IN YOUR INVESTING

REAL ESTATE ASSOCIATIONS

Local Real Estate Investor Associations (REIA Groups)

Across the country, local groups of investors have come together to form investor associations. These groups typically meet once a month at a local venue and discuss items of importance to the member investors. For a state-by-state listing of local groups, go to *www.ResultsNow.com* and click on the link for "Investor Groups."

American Real Estate Investors Association (AREIA)

The American Real Estate Investors Association is a nationwide group of real estate investors who have joined to help each other and themselves be more successful in their investing. AREIA not only gives its members the chance to network with other success-minded investors, but it also provides them with ongoing training and support. AREIA is a "virtual" investor group; its members meet through conference calls and over the Web on their members-only website.

It's interesting to note that most AREIA members also belong to their local investor group. AREIA members have greatly benefited by having access to investors in other areas of the country, too. Whether these investors are just more willing to share because they don't view the other members as local competition or simply because different areas are the breeding grounds for new ideas, AREIA members benefit greatly from this free exchange of ideas. For more information on joining AREIA, visit the association's website at *www.americanreia.com*.

NINE MUST-READ BOOKS FOR REAL ESTATE INVESTORS

- *Making Big Money Investing in Real Estate Without Tenants, Banks, or Rehab Projects*—a great companion to this book (Conti)
- *Rich Dad, Poor Dad* (Kiyosaki and Lechter)
- *Secrets of a Millionaire Real Estate Investor* (Shemin)
- *Influence: The Psychology of Persuasion* (Cialdini)
- *Guaranteed Millionaire* (Phillips)
- *Investing in Real Estate,* Fourth Edition (McLean and Eldred)
- *How I Raised Myself from Failure to Success in Selling* (Bettger)
- *The Real Estate Investor's Answer Book* (Cummings)
- *Flipping Properties* (Bronchick and Dahlstrom)

HOME STUDY COURSES

Over the past 10 years, Peter and The Success Team have created several step-by-step home study courses for investors. Each course is composed of a combination of CDs, DVDs, and manuals; most of them include a CD-ROM of forms and contracts.

To find out more about any of the following courses or grab some free investor resources, visit our website at *www.ResultsNow.com.*

"The Protégé Program: The Complete Buying Without Cash or Credit Home-Study Course"—These are the same materials used in The Mentoring Program. With the 5 manuals and 36 CDs, thousands of clients have discovered the secrets to buying nice homes without cash or credit.

"How to Find, Close, and Sell Properties 'Subject to' the Existing Financing"—This is a masters course that was created specifically for investors who want to specialize in buying properties "subject to" the existing financing.

"How to Create Massive Streams of Cash Flow with Multi-Units"—Learning how to determine the value of apartment buildings quickly is one of the first sections in this training. This course goes on to show you how to find multiunit deals, how to manage, increase the value, and sell at top dollar.

"The Advanced Business Systems and Strategies Training"—This course is recommended specifically for Level Two investors. The focus is on mastering the five core skills and using leverage to systematize your investing business.

"Negotiate and Grow Rich: Advanced Negotiating Strategies: How to Handle Every Negotiation You'll Ever Face as a Real Estate Investor"—Negotiating is the highest-paying skill you will ever develop. No investing library is complete without this course, which has been referred to as the "negotiator's bible."

"How to Buy Foreclosures Without Cash or Credit—Advanced Foreclosure Investing Strategies"—This course was created when we did a live three-day training for our advanced clients. In this book, we were only able to cover about the first 5 to 10 minutes of each 2-hour to 3-hour session of the live training session. This course contains everything we knew at the time regarding foreclosure investing along with warnings and tips from some of our most successful clients.

LIVE WORKSHOPS

In addition to these home study courses, we host several intensive, multiday workshops on various investing topics including foreclosures, negotiating, and commercial investing. For information on the Ultimate Investors Bootcamp and other live training sessions, go to *www.ResultsNow.com*.

MENTORSHIP PROGRAM

Each year, we work with a handful of investors in a comprehensive year-long program teaching them how to achieve success in real estate investing. The program offers daily access to expert coaching and personalized help through every step of their deals. This program is designed for individuals who are *committed to* achieving investment success in the shortest possible time. To find out more or to apply for this program, go to *www.ResultsNow.com* and click on "Mentorship Program" or call toll-free 800-825-0215.

COMMERCIAL MENTORING

This program is limited to those investors who want to work with the highest tier of Success Team Coaches, including Peter

Conti and Peter Harris, to learn how to raise funds and invest in big deals such as the following:

- Multiunits and apartment buildings
- Office buildings and retail
- Warehouse and industrial properties
- Shopping centers
- Land development

To find out more or to apply for this program, go to *www.ResultsNow.com* and click on "Commercial Mentoring" or call toll-free 800-825-0215.

WEBSITES TO HELP YOU WITH YOUR INVESTING

www.ResultsNow.com—Site hosted by The Success Team containing free investor resources and articles

www.americanreia.com—Lots of useful information on national and links to local real estate investor organizations around the country

www.creonline.com—Great discussion groups and investing articles

www.resales.usda.gov/properties.cfm—Information on government-owned real estate for sale

www.treas.gov/auctions/irs/index.html—Information on IRS-seized property being auctioned off

www.inman.com—Great real estate articles and information featuring syndicated columnist and attorney Robert Bruss

www.legalwiz.com—Great site on legal aspects of investing

www.bankrate.com—Mortgage rates from Bankrate.com

www.list.realestate.yahoo.com/re/neighborhood/main.html—Useful site through Yahoo to find home values and neighborhood information *www.census.gov*—Access to detailed census data, down to zip code level

www.mbaa.org/consumer/—Consumer section of Mortgage Bankers Association of America; useful calculators and planning tools

www.myfico.com—Information on your credit score

www.financenter.com/—Best mortgage and financial planning tools on the Internet

www.propertydisposal.gsa.gov/property/—Information on government auctions, including real estate

www.hud.gov/offices/hsg/sfh/reo/homes.cfm—Information on HUD foreclosures for sale and other programs they have available

Self-made multimillionaire Peter Conti and his Success Team are the nation's leading real estate investment experts. Peter and each of his hand-picked Success Coaches are successful business owners, investors, and passionate trainers.

Peter is the author of *How to Create Multiple Streams of Income Buying Homes in Nice Areas with Nothing Down*, which was selected as one of the all-time top three investing books by the American Real Estate Investors Association. His second book, *Making Big Money Investing in Real Estate Without Tenants, Banks, or Rehab Projects*, was chosen as a "Top 10 Pick" by syndicated columnist Robert Bruss. *Making Big Money Investing in Foreclosures Without Cash or Credit* skyrocketed to success on the *Wall Street Journal* best seller list and prompted the publisher to ask Peter and his Success Team to write this second edition.

Each year, The Mentor Family holds workshops and reunions at which thousands of investors across the country continue to discover the realities of making money by investing in real estate. The Success Team's real estate holdings are valued at over $100 million. Students in the Program have bought and sold over $1 billion worth of real estate over the past decade. Peter mentored the Success Team of the original San Diego Challenge in which he guided a group of three novice investors to pick up more than $1.5 million worth of properties—with only $37 down.

For more information, visit *www.ResultsNow.com* or contact the Success Team at

Mentor Financial Group, LLC
7475 W. 5th Ave., Suite 100
Lakewood, CO 80226
Email: *mentor@ResultsNow.com*
800-825-0215